A DEADLY ROSE

A Romance Thriller Novel

K.R. Wrights

JOURNAL JOY
An Imprint of Journal Joy Publishers

For Publishing Information, contact Journal Joy at Info@thejournaljoy.com.

www.thejournaljoy.com

Paperback ISBN: 978-1-957751-77-1

Editor: Nicole Gyimah

First paperback edition, 2023

CONTENTS

CHAPTER 1
Beginning to an End

———❧———

I packed up the last of my things and threw them into my book bag. I quickly wrapped the charger cord around my laptop and shoved it into my bag to make sure I didn't leave it behind, making a mental note to buy a laptop case the next time I was out. I was starting to notice the scratches on my laptop from my keys brushing against the surface in my backpack. My laptop was barely surviving as it is between the falls, viruses, and worn-out cord.

I paused briefly to glance around the room. It felt empty—still filled with his cologne, clothes, and shoes, but empty. Suddenly, a moment of déjà vu: I've stood in this place before, bag in my hand, deciding to leave and thinking through my next steps. Am I doing the right thing? Did I forget anything? What is my next move? Over the last few days, I had calculated everything down to a tee. I emptied drawers and closets little by little and replaced my things with old clothes I no longer wore. Some of the clothes were not even mine; they were his. But he hadn't noticed. I'd been packing meticulously just to make sure I didn't leave anything behind—or maybe because I didn't really want to leave.

I glanced around the room again, closing my eyes to reflect on some of the good memories. Were there really any of those? Looking at the clock, 9:27 a.m., I speed up my movements so I could leave in the next five minutes, tops! My goal was to be on the road by 9:30 a.m. after most of the rush hour ended. I checked the closets and drawers again, then started removing my perfume bottles and makeup from the dresser. I do not need an excuse to come back here and get sucked back into this mess again.

I look at the clock again; 9:34 a.m. Damn, so much for five minutes. I tossed the remaining items from the dresser into my purse in one quick sweep, dropping half of them on the floor, including my Chapstick and a pair of diamond studded earrings.

"Crap." Five minutes just turned into ten.

I watched as everything scattered under the bed and the dresser. One by one, I collected everything, stretching my arms to try and move the earrings back in my direction. Of course, they rolled to the farthest and darkest corner under the dresser. Even with my long arms, I knew they had gone into places where I couldn't reach. Ten minutes turned into fifteen. I felt myself becoming exasperated with every effort. I kept trying and accidentally pushed my earrings further away as I tried to grab them.

Fifteen minutes now and counting.

"Fuck it."

2

I gave up. They are better off under the dresser, anyway, or in the trash, I thought. I got back up, wiped the dust off my sleeve, and accidentally hit my hip against the dresser, knocking over a picture frame on the floor.

The glass shattered, revealing broken pieces over smiling faces in the picture underneath it. I stared at the picture for a moment and wondered if I should clean up the glass. The more I stared at the broken pieces on the floor, the more I realized that it was an accurate depiction of our lives over the past few years, smiling through the lies, broken promises, and false narratives. I bent down to pick up the picture, then suddenly stopped. What am I going to do with it? I walked over to the nightstand, on what used to be my side of the bed, leaving the broken frame on the floor behind me for him to find. Frustrated at the thought that I now must buy a new pair of earrings on top of furniture and a new place, I grabbed my charger and headed out of the bedroom to go downstairs.

I looked around the living room and checked the spare office just to make sure I didn't leave any miscellaneous junk lying around. The hallways were filled with pictures from vacations, his family cookouts, galas, and fundraisers that we'd attended over the years. I tried not to look at the photos as I roamed the halls and spare rooms in silence, looking for the last of my things. This would be my last time in this townhouse that I shared with my now ex-fiancé, Jeff. After the last episode of humiliation due to his cheating, which resulted in the second pregnancy rumor, it was finally time for me to go—though it wasn't a rumor, as Jeff would have liked for me to believe. The pregnancy was real. Part of me knew that the rumors in the past were always real. I guess the universe got tired of me ignoring the warning signs.

Two weeks prior, I'd seen a text on Jeff's phone from someone named "Emi."

★★★★

Emi: "I just took the third test, Jeff. I'm pregnant, and it's yours. Stop ignoring me and call me back!"

I continued scrolling and saw the confirmation picture of a hand holding a pregnancy test with a positive sign. I remembered staring at the picture and forgetting to breathe, feeling like I had been kicked in the stomach, again. The sting of tears rose in my eyes as I reread the proof of Jeff's betrayal through a text. So far, all I knew of this "Emi" was that she had well-manicured nails and a green emerald ring on her index finger. I noticed the ring because it was a princess cut emerald with a diamond halo around it. I didn't care for halos, but this one was gorgeous, at least 3.5 carats. I could tell right away that she was wealthy, or whoever purchased the ring had been. I learned a lot about diamonds over the years from being around Jeff, his family, and their jewelry empire, so I could tell this one cost a pretty penny.

Even then while looking at the text and the picture, I was praying that this wasn't the truth. I kept hoping that this was some sort of mistake, and the next text would be Jeff saying, "I'm sorry. You have the wrong number." Instead, his response was:

Jeff: "Are you sure? I thought you were on the pill! You know we can't have a baby. You need to get rid of it."

Emi: "You know I won't do that. Answer your phone! We need to meet now!"

We? They were awe. When did my fiancé become a we with someone else? And how long was this we going on? And now, the we, excluding me, were about to have a baby. More importantly, he hadn't denied it. I was staring at proof of his infidelity right there through a text on his phone, which meant I couldn't deny it, either. I knew all the other times were true, too, but there was never any proof; not like this. This was something that I couldn't ignore and pretend was a bad dream. He had gotten her pregnant, and he couldn't deny it or lie to me this time. He couldn't say she was lying, or "I don't even know that girl." A part of me wanted to be upset with Emi, blaming her for the pain I felt, his lies, and our failed relationship. But she was innocent. Whether she knew about me or not, she wasn't the person I was in a relationship with. She wasn't the one who promised to be loyal when he proposed. And from the look of the text, Emi was dealing with a different kind of pain from my own.

The man she was sleeping with was ignoring her and telling her to get rid of their child. He hadn't denied them sleeping together, just their future. I wanted to feel bad for her, but my own hurt and anger grew inside of me. The fact is he was sleeping with her, without the courtesy of a condom, and she was pregnant with their child.

I checked the clock in the foyer. 9:48 a.m.

I headed toward the basement door, remembering that I had clothes in the dryer. I hate coming down here; it's always been the creepiest place in the house. I walked down the stairs and headed towards the washer and dryer while the rest of the space echoed darkness behind me. Jeff kept a spare room in the back for his martial arts practice, but other than that, the space was empty. I offered to turn it into a man cave for him once, but he declined, stating that "only boys needed caves to make them feel like men." At the time, I thought it was his way of always being close to me in our home. Ours. I chuckled at the thought. This place had never been ours.

I opened the dryer to check my clothes and, of course, they weren't dry. Slamming the door shut, I hit the "quick dry" button to restart the dryer. I checked my watch—9:52 a.m. Great.

CHAPTER 2
Mr. Popular

———⟨∾⟩———

I headed back upstairs to make a sandwich while I waited, realizing now how uncomfortable it was to be in this house surrounded by memories. I'd stuck by Jeff and his nonsense for six long years. He had always been promiscuous, so cheating on me was nothing new for him.

We met during my sophomore year. He was Mr. Popular, so I avoided him on campus most of the time, since I was the introvert with only two or three close friends. Jeff had all the attributes the girls at school admired: smart, ambitious, funny, and family-oriented. I later found out he possessed none of these at all. He was tall, handsome, and had a slick smile that could pass for sexy or sinister depending on how he used it. Unfortunately, he was also a liar—a terrible, pathological liar. This often led to him trying to cover up his cheating with other women.

Jeff majored in finance, with a minor in *women's studies*. I smile thinking about how much he hates that joke. Every other month, there was a new girl on his arm. I used to watch him hop around campus with his fraternity brothers and noticed how, even without ever saying a word, he could drive women crazy. And

8

even though he had options, he still pursued me, making little remarks about us getting married whenever we saw each other in class, offering to buy my groceries, and volunteering himself to drive me places off campus when I didn't have a ride. For a while, it all just felt like harmless flirting, and I thought I knew better than to believe anything that came out of his mouth.

One year, a storm hit our campus and destroyed half of the city. My roommate lived close enough that she was able to go home for the weekend before the storm hit, but I was stuck there, as I didn't have a car. She offered for me to come with her, but I didn't think the storm would be that bad. The people in the south usually panicked over minor weather conditions anyway. Now, stuck in my dorm without any food or company, I logged into Facebook to look through pictures and status updates. A message notification popped up: "Jeffrey R. sent you a message." Strange—we had never exchanged words outside of our thirty-second banters while passing each other on campus. Reluctantly, I opened the message expecting to see another one of his sexual advances, but he simply said:

"Hey, Kamren . . . How are you? Hope the storm is treating you okay."

Overlooking the fact that he misspelled my name, even though I spelled it correctly on my profile, I was intrigued to see him interact like a caring human being. After about an hour of chatting, Jeff insisted on bringing me something to eat after I told him I ran out of snacks. Twenty minutes later, he was at my dorm with food and my favorite chocolate. He only lived seven minutes away, but the storm flooded some of the main streets. We sat in the dorm lobby and talked for almost an hour while sharing a meal. I could feel my infatuation for him growing.

"Why did you come all the way over here just to bring me food, Jeff?"

"You only live a few minutes away, so why not? We both need to eat," he responded.

"You know what I mean. What do you want?" I insisted.

"Well, I think it's obvious that I like you and wanted to spend some time with you."

"Hmph. Is that right?" I asked sarcastically.

"Do you like me?" he asked, flashing his sexy smile through his pearly whites.

"Everyone likes you, Jeff. What does it matter if I do or don't?"

"It just does." He leaned toward me from his chair. "You're the only one who matters."

Then, he kissed me, and all of the butterflies from every encounter we ever had come flooding in my stomach. He had me hooked with one kind gesture and a kiss.

"So, what now?" he asked, after he finally released my lips.

I blinked back into reality and glanced around the lobby. No one was there to witness our passionate moment, besides the news anchor on the 19-inch television hanging from the wall.

"You go home. The storm is finally calming down." *Inside and outside*, I thought.

"You sure?"

"Yes. Let's not ruin the moment."

"You see, that's why I like you." He kissed me again and stood up to head out.

We didn't date initially, but after a few months, I finally gave in. We started dating my junior year and his *super*-senior year in college. I figured by then that he would've outgrown his habit of chasing multiple women, assuming most college guys had matured by their senior year and were able to be in a committed relationship. Little did I know that most guys hadn't outgrown that phase of having scattered ass all around campus. At least, Jeff hadn't.

Even back in college, there were signs that he couldn't be faithful. And, like a true fool, I forgave him every time, even after getting wind that he got a girl pregnant in college before we graduated. He begged, pleaded, and said he made a mistake and cheated, but he didn't get the girl pregnant. He was positive that the baby wasn't his, claiming that the girl only wanted to pin it on him because she knew he could provide financially.

Most people knew that Jeff was born into money—old money. While most college kids worked or watched their parents struggle to pay for tuition, Jeff lived the life of luxury. Even though freshmen weren't allowed to have cars, Jeff had one. His parents made him live on campus for his first year to gain the college experience, but by his sophomore year, he had his own apartment off campus with no roommates. This made it easier for him to have as many women as possible whenever he wanted. He convinced his parents that campus parties were a distraction, so they didn't mind him living off campus and paying for his apartment. But I suspect Jeff told them that lie after he kept getting caught sneaking girls out of his dorm room after the curfew.

Even with all the money, Jeff never seemed satisfied with what he had. I often noticed two different sides to him. One was the humble and generous side that he showed his friends, which is why everyone loved him and the girls flocked to him like bees to honey. Then, there was the aggressive and temperamental side he displayed when things didn't go his way. I always suspected it had a lot to do with the strained relationship between him and his family, a topic he quickly avoided whenever it came up.

Ironically, now, as I look around the living room of this beautifully decorated townhouse, I didn't feel angry or sad about leaving. In the past, I would have been so distraught over Jeff's lies and the constant fights that I would think of any reason at all just to stay. Even back then, I was tired of arguing, questioning him, feeling insecure, and still being lied to. So, yes, I was stupid then, but not anymore. I always managed to convince myself that I loved him and wanted to make the relationship work. And I believed he loved me, too, at one point. Over the years, there were plenty of ups and downs, but Ms. Emerald Ring was the final straw.

I walked back downstairs to the basement and stopped the dryer mid-cycle. I felt my clothes to check for dampness; finally, they were dry. I headed back upstairs and tried to stuff them into my already overpacked suitcases. I scribbled a note, stuck it on the fridge, grabbed my keys off the hallway table, and headed for the door. Passing the hall clock, I took a last glance: *10:12 a.m.* I thought about tossing the keys in the trash on my way out, but thought, What good would that do? I guess it would be polite if I locked the door on my way out. I closed the front door, double checking to make sure it was locked, threw the last of my bags in the back seat of my car, and hopped in the driver's seat. After all the crying, all I could do was stare as I looked up at the windows to the townhouse. It had never really felt like home to me, even though I tried to incorporate pieces of me throughout the years.

I moved in with Jeff a year after I graduated, remembering how happy I was when he asked me to move in. I had been spending most of my nights there, so it felt only natural that living together was the next step. He suggested that I leave clothes at his house and cleaned out half of his closet and drawer space. He placed a key in a velvet black box and gave it to me over dinner one night. Silly me; I took that as a sign that our relationship had progressed to a better place. I was hopeful that all the cheating was behind us, since we were now living under the same roof. Yeah, right.

I backed out of the parking space and stopped at the end of the driveway to remove "Kamryn Hanover" from the mailbox, finally feeling a sense of freedom for the first time. But this freedom also came with a healthy dose of loneliness. I was leaving a relationship with nothing but the impression that I was going nowhere. When I finally decided to leave Jeff, I realized I didn't really have a plan B. Our life together was my only plan for a long while. Thankfully, my mother suggested I come back home in the meantime until I found a place. Her exact words were, "Screw him! You don't have to stay there and be uncomfortable because he's a cheater! Just come home."

Car clock: 10:19 a.m.

My mom lived about an hour away, but if the highways were backed up due to construction or an accident, it could take me up

14

to two hours. I was thankful that she lived close enough that I could drive, since I technically had no place else to go. I always thought Jeff bought this place just for the distance. My mom's house had been my only home before I moved out for college, so part of me was happy about moving home. The other part of me couldn't shake the feeling of being a failure. I never planned to move back home; at least, not like this.

CHAPTER 3
Work, work, work...

After almost forty-five minutes on the road, I felt like I was still closer to Jeff's place than home. With still no sign of what was causing this traffic, I reached for the radio knob to rummage through the stations. Love songs. I sighed, irritated by the choices. I saw the universe was up to its old tricks again. I changed the dial again and "F.N.F." by Glo Rilla was on. I smiled at the message and turned the volume up. My cell phone started ringing, and I could tell from the ringtone who it was—Jeff.

This morning, Jeff woke up, showered, and dressed as usual. When he was fully dressed, he walked over to my side of the bed and asked me if I was going to work. "No" was my only reply as I lay in bed pretending to still be asleep. He accepted my answer and didn't ask me any more questions. He leaned down to kiss me and rubbed the side of my face; I cringed. He whispered how sorry he was for hurting me again and that he loved me. His last words before he left were, "Kamryn, I promise I'll make it up to you. Let's have dinner tonight at the Italian place you like."

He always knew he could win me over with a satisfying meal. He also knew I loved Italian food. That's what I get for being so greedy. But how he planned to make it up to me while someone else was carrying his child, I would never know. When I didn't respond to his dinner invitation, I heard his footsteps pause before he left the room and headed out the front door. Once he was gone, I hopped out of bed and started getting ready to load my car with luggage. Jeff had no clue. I had been packing my things for two weeks, and he didn't even notice. All the closets and drawers were emptied of my things, except for a few pieces that I wore during the week. I wondered what his reaction would be when he came home tonight to find my note on the refrigerator:

"Can't make it to dinner tonight… or any other night."

It's the least I could do. I ignored the ringtone and continued to press through traffic.

I had less than two weeks before starting my new job, so the time off would be good.

It was time for me to move on from Dean & Associates. Anyway, I arranged for a few vacation days after giving my notice from work to move my things and get settled. I needed to start focusing on my career and getting back into the marketing world. After four years with little to no movement towards my professional ambitions, I knew that my chances of further advancement there were slim to none. When I gave Mr. Harold my two weeks' notice, he pretended to be shocked.

****

"You're leaving??? I thought you were interested in working in our new offices downtown! Why would you quit?" Harold asked.

"I am interested, but not as a bookkeeper. I appreciate the opportunity you gave me here, but I want to focus more on my degree. You know, marketing?"

"What? You can't do that here?"

I sighed. Trying to convince Mr. Harold of anything was nearly impossible. He was a master at persuasion, which was how I ended up doing bookkeeping and accounting for his legal firm for the past few years.

Harold Dean was an old friend of the family. He and my dad met in the early '90s when they worked at the same law firm. He ended up leaving the firm to care for his wife, Marlene, when she had taken ill. Marlene and my mother had bonded over the years. When your husbands are busy lawyers and work late most nights, you tend to have a lot in common. Unfortunately, the one thing they didn't have in common was that my dad spent most of his late nights in his office with his secretary. When my mom finally caught on, it had been a seven-year relationship that produced a four-year-old love child. Naturally, my mother was devastated, but Angela Hanover wasn't a chump. She made sure that she and I were taken care of in the aftermath of the divorce. And my dad didn't fight it, which helped. Ms. Marlene offered her support throughout the entire process, while Mr. Harold refused to represent either party due to their friendship.

Once Ms. Marlene became ill, it was my mother's turn to offer her support. After she passed, Mr. Harold decided to start his own firm. Shortly after I graduated, my mother reached out and asked him if he needed any help around the firm. He laughed, saying how he could barely afford to pay someone to answer the phone. But Harold, being the kind soul that he was, agreed to hire me and give me whatever title I wanted if I accepted the salary he could afford. Luckily for me, I was desperately looking for work.

"I really do appreciate that, Mr. Harold. Really, I do. But I think it's time for me to focus on media marketing full-time. Plus, Ted is fully capable of taking over my responsibilities. And you know I'll come help whenever you need."

"Ted!" Mr. Harold screamed. "That kid can barely send a fax. I wouldn't trust him with my files or books; you know that."

"He's ready, Mr. Harold. He's been with us for eight months now, and he knows everything I know. Trust me: He's ready for more. He just needs a little TLC." I chuckled at Mr. Harold as he rolled his eyes. "I promise I'll come back and visit and to help out whenever you need."

"Yeah, yeah. Get out of here. Good luck, kid."

I started preparing Ted for my job right after that, which left little time for me to prepare for my new job. I'd just accepted an offer for an Assistant Director of Marketing position at a top advertising agency, Alpine Bloom Advertising. Sarah Alpine, the CEO, was a guest speaker at a marketing seminar I attended last summer, and I had been obsessed with her ever since. We attended the same alma mater, but she majored in marketing and journalism. I read in an article that once she realized people weren't going to feature her work or listen to her ideas, she knew she had to start her own company.

I stalked her company's LinkedIn profile for six months before I saw that the Assistant Marketing Director position had opened up. I debated over the decision to send my resume in for two weeks before I worked up enough courage to press send. I was keeping up with the latest industry news, completed my master's program, and assisted Mr. Harold with small marketing strategies over the years, so I felt prepared. However, ten minutes after I clicked send, I received an email letting me know that the position had been filled and was no longer available.

Disappointed, I called Jeff to share the news, looking for him to feasibly comfort me. He pretended to feel bad for ten seconds and reassured me that I didn't have to worry about work, suggesting that I take up media marketing as a hobby and not a career. Good old Jeff, The ultimate dream encourager. I recall that day because it was right around the holidays, and Jeff had started working late again. Not unusual, but around this time, his company kept the workload light so that employees could spend more time with their families. So, why was he working late a week before Christmas? I shrugged off the notion that he might be cheating and continued my online search for work.

A few months later, I received an email from Alpine Bloom Advertising asking me to come in for an interview. I rolled my eyes at the email, thinking that they must want to offer me a job as their coffee runner, since I had no business trying to be their Assistant Director of Marketing. To my surprise, it was for the same position, which was somehow now available again. I typed my reply email so fast that I had to reread it six times to catch all the grammatical errors my excitement caused.

I remembered calling Jeff immediately to tell him the good news. No answer. He never answered while he was at work. Instead, I called my best friend, Mica, to share my good news. She answered on the first ring.

"Hey, girl, hey!" Mica exclaimed. That was our greeting since high school.

"Mica! Guess what?!" I tried to hold on to my excitement.

"Girl, who . . ."

"They called me in for an interview!" I screamed.

"AHHHHH! See?! I told you! Congrats, Kamryn! Now, stop screaming, and tell me who called you in and for what."

"Michelle, you know the job at the Alpine company as the Assistant Marketing Director."

Michelle Canmore, affectionately known as Mica, had the worst memory known to man. I'd only been talking about Alpine Bloom for ten months.

"Apparently, the job just opened back up, and they're only interviewing a few people who applied last time. And I'm one of the few! AHHHHH!"

"Oh, my God! Congrats! That's so exciting. And when you get the job, because you most definitely will, we can go to lunch together, since you'll be closer."

"Yes! I'm so excited for the interview that I can barely focus. I wonder what happened to—"

The line clicked, and I paused to look at my phone. "Mica, it's Jeff. Let me call you back."

I could hear Mica rolling her eyes through the phone, but all she let out was, "Mm-hmm . . . Call me later. Bye."

I clicked over to the other line.

"Jeff?"

"Hey. What's up? You called?"

"Yeah. I wanted to tell you some good news."

"Oh, yeah? What's that?" he asked in a tone that told me he wasn't having a good day.

"Are you okay? You seem upset."

"I'm fine, Kamryn. Just busy. What do you have to tell me?"

"Well, I heard back from . . ."

"Hold on." Jeff put his hand over the phone to stop me from hearing the female voice in the background. As intelligent as this man was, he still didn't know how to work the mute or hold buttons on his phone.

He came back to the line after a few seconds. "Hey. Can we talk about this later tonight? I have a client emergency."

"Sure. What time will you be home later? Maybe I can fix us some dinner."

"Uh, I'm not sure. I'll probably just grab something to eat around the office if I'm here late. I'll let you know."

Ten days in a row, he had been working late. I was starting to lose my patience with this man.

"You're working late again? Seems kind of strange."

"Strange? What's strange about working late and making money? You already know how hectic my job can be."

"Yes, but it's the holiday—"

"Kamryn, I don't have time for this right now. We'll talk later, okay? I need to go."

The line ended, and suddenly, my good news didn't feel so great. I hated it when he cut me off like that and dictated when we would talk. That night, he didn't come home until 2:30 in the morning. The next day, he didn't remember to ask me about my news or offer to explain his arrival home during booty-call hours. I decided to keep my news to myself until after the interview.

The interview was scheduled for a Saturday because they were trying to fit all the candidates in quickly. I was already nervous since a whole week had gone by, and I was probably one of the last candidates to be seen and the least qualified. I was sure that by now, they must have interviewed someone who was better suited for the job. When I arrived, Sarah was standing near the reception desk looking through her phone. I stopped in my tracks, suddenly nervous at seeing her right in front of me. She looked up when she heard the elevator bell and approached me.

"Hi! You must be Ms. Kamryn Hanover, correct?"

"Yes." That was all I could say.

"Great! I'm Sarah Alpine. Thank you so much for coming in to meet me on a Saturday." She extended her hand for me to shake.

"No problem at all. Thank you for seeing me, Ms. Alpine." I could feel my palms starting to sweat and a lump forming in my throat as I stood face-to-face with the CEO of Alpine Bloom Advertising. She was tall, beautiful, in great shape, and gracious. She even smelled nice. The entire building smelled like peonies and hydrangeas.

"Please, call me Sarah. It's just going to be us today, so we might as well get acquainted. I didn't want to make my entire staff come in on Saturday because of my hectic schedule."

I could see she was thoughtful, too; yes, I could definitely work for her. I followed her down the hall and tried to straighten my blouse and hair in the reflection of the glass doors as I walked behind her. I usually have a few minutes before an interview to do these last-minute checks in the bathroom. I wiped my teeth with my tongue to remove any lipstick stains right before we walked into her office.

The interview lasted for two hours. Startlingly, we talked very little about my work at Dean & Associates and more about our alma mater. She was intrigued about my experiences and how much the school had changed since she graduated ten years before me. When we finally did look over my resume, I confessed that I hadn't spent much time in the marketing field as I would have liked, but I expressed my confidence in being able to do the job. She glanced over the resume one more time before looking back at me.

"Why do you want to be in this field?" she asked quietly.

I thought about it for a few seconds, wondering if I should give my honest feeling or an answer better suited for the position.

"I love bringing life to things. That's what marketing and advertising is for me: influencing the perception around the idea of a product and bringing life to businesses. For me, it's about adding color and character to the world," I answered honestly.

Sarah smiled. "Interesting."

I rushed home from my interview to tell Jeff that I was offered the job. He didn't even know I was still looking, since we had barely talked due to his late hours. It was still early enough that we could go out and celebrate. I walked in the front door and called for him.

"Jeff! Honey, where are you?"

No answer. I ran upstairs to check the bedroom, thinking he was probably still in bed from working so late. I walked into the bedroom—no Jeff. I heard the shower water turn on from the hall. I knocked on the door and walked in.

"Hey, honey. I'm surprised to see you up."

"Hey, baby." He poked his head from behind the shower curtain. "I wanted to get up early so I could play some golf and go into the office."

"Seriously, Jeff? On a Saturday?"

"Yes, Kamryn. What's wrong with golf?" He asked like he didn't know what I was talking about.

"I'm talking about work, Jeff. Why do you need to go in today?"

"I told you I had a client emergency, so things are a little busier than normal. Can you close the door? I'll be out in a sec."

Dismissed, again. I stormed out of the bathroom, annoyed all over again. Late nights and now weekends. I sat on the side of the bed and took off my heels, realizing that any plans I had for today with him were over. Jeff's phone started to buzz on the dresser. He always had it with him, so I was surprised he left it in the room while he took a shower. Most likely, it was because I hadn't been home. The buzzing continued. Undoubtedly work. Could be his new client calling him about that "emergency." I grabbed the phone just as it stopped vibrating. It was unlocked, and I saw missed calls from someone named "Emi." I considered looking through his phone to check for myself. Even though that's never been my style, I wondered when I would ever get another chance to get real answers to pending suspicions.

I went to the home screen to find his text messages and started reading. For a few seconds, I was in shock. Then, I felt what could only be described as someone kicking me in the stomach repeatedly. I felt my throat get tight, and tears formed in my eyes. I wanted to scream and cry out, but as I opened my mouth, nothing came out. I heard the bathroom door open and Jeff's footsteps as he walked into the bedroom.

"Babe, I thought you were running errands this morning. Why are you so dressed up?"

He stopped dead in his tracks when he saw me standing there holding his phone . . . reading his secrets.

I looked up at him and stared for what seemed like an hour but was probably three seconds. I could tell he was waiting for my next move. He looked worried or unsure if I was going to cry, scream, or attack.

"Who's Emi?"

CHAPTER 4
Mrs. Hanover

When I called my mother to let her know that we broke up and I was leaving him, she made a poor attempt to hide her excitement. Angela Hanover wasn't too fond of Jeff, and her contempt towards him had become harder to disguise over the years. She immediately insisted that I come back home that night and stay with her. That was a few weeks ago, and she had grown impatient.

After another forty-five minutes in traffic, the universe finally decided to play fair. I was less than ten minutes away when I noticed a car switching lanes behind me that looked exactly like Jeff's silver BMW. A sudden panic rose in my chest. Is he following me? How did he know I was driving here? I slowed down slightly to wait for the driver to pass me so I could catch a quick glimpse. I let out a sigh of relief. Not him.

As I pulled in front of my mother's house, I felt a sudden twinge of emptiness. I had no intentions of going back to Jeff, but fear had finally found its way to my heart and had me thinking I should turn back around. Turning off the car, I unbuckled my seat belt and threw my keys in my purse. If I just kept moving forward, maybe I would stop yearning to go back.

****

"I don't understand why you stayed there so long," my mother stated.

I shifted my gaze towards the window and tried to think of another topic. My mother was one of the kindest souls in the world, but she was also a force to be reckoned with if you messed with her daughter. She had been more infuriated over the recent events than I was. We never discussed my relationship in detail over the years. She knew about the past indiscretions and grew increasingly distant toward Jeff over the years.

"He was an asshole. I told him many years ago to never hurt you or break your heart. And now this, again?!" Angela was almost screaming her words out.

"It's fine, Mom. It was over long before this. I can't keep repeating the same cycle with him expecting things to change. It's finally done." I said it loud enough to convince myself.

"I just hate to see you so upset and hurt like this. You deserve someone who's going to treat you with respect. And you'll get that soon enough. I'm just glad you're back at home. You know how much I always miss you."

"I missed you, too, Mom. I'll try not to be too much of a burden while I'm here."

"Oh, please, stop it. What burden is it to have my daughter home with me?"

"You deserve to have your own space and privacy, too, Mom. You raised me to be independent, not to rely on anyone." I groaned. "I feel so helpless."

"Now, that's enough. You better stop talking about yourself like that. I don't like it," Angela snapped.

"I'm just saying . . ."

"I mean it, Kamryn Angela Hanover. That's enough. You're human, and you are bound to make mistakes. There's nothing wrong with loving a man who you believe loves you back. We've all been there. Hell, some of us more than others." My mother rolled her eyes at what I assumed was a flashback to her own young love life with my dad.

"You just have to learn how to love yourself more and remember not to lose yourself. You might feel like you stayed around too long, but that's okay. You're here now. Life isn't over, and this is not the end. You're a smart, beautiful woman who's done some dumb things. But that's life, sweetheart. Life is about living, losing, and learning how to live again."

My mother, the saint, always had a way with words. She could bring comfort to me in any situation, always honest, direct, and loving in her approach. And when I needed a stern kick in the butt, she could deliver that, too.

"Thanks, Mom."

Attempting to hold my tears back was proving to be of no use. This morning, I felt like Wonder Woman when I left the townhouse, but now, sitting here talking to my mother made me feel like a ten-year-old girl.

"It's going to be okay, sweetheart," Angela said.

"I just feel so dumb, like the village idiot who everyone knew was getting cheated on, except for me. I've wondered if every pregnant woman I've passed in the street for the last few weeks could be her."

Angela chuckled. "Kamryn, you only feel that way because that's how you feel about yourself right now. You're feeling vulnerable and highly sensitive. You just ended an era of your life, and you are preparing to enter uncharted territory—no fiancé, a new job, and, soon, a new place. So, you're trying to figure all of that out without having that knucklehead around. He was your safety net, sweetie, which is why you stayed so long."

She was right again.

"But I promise you, you are not alone. I am here for you, and so are the rest of your friends. There's nothing wrong with having to lean on loved ones for a little help and encouragement from time to time."

"Feels like I've been leaning for years. I should be able to stand by now." With those few words, I felt my strength slipping away.

"Says who?" Angela asked.

I chuckled a little at my mother's quick response. "Says everyone. Society. I've been out of the house since college, practically, and I have nothing to show for it. I'm supposed to be independent, and here I am, crawling back home because I broke up with my fiancé."

"You didn't crawl, Kamryn. You walked. And it's about time you did. Do you think you're the only person in the world who's broken up with a man and had to start over?"

I shrugged my shoulders, unable to cultivate a proper sentence.

"Well, you're not." Angela's voice trailed off. I realized that I'd hit a soft spot for my mom.

"What if you had been married to that man or had children with him?" Angela shivered at the thought. "I say count your blessings and be thankful you were able to walk away without any baggage."

"I'm sorry, Mom." I have to admit it now, but I did want children with Jeff; at one point, we almost had a child.

"There's no shame in having to come home, sweetheart. And I know you're being hard on yourself right now and feeling sad. But you can't stay that way forever. Your attitude and emotions will eventually affect everything that you do. So, try not to feel sad for too long. I'll give you forty-eight hours to get all your tears out. And then, after that, I want to see my confident, sweet daughter walking around." Angela smiled, hugged, and kissed me on the cheek.

"Only forty-eight hours, Mom? Gee, that's mighty generous of you," I responded sarcastically.

"You're lucky I gave you that much." Angela smiled.

I tried to give my most genuine smile as I hugged my mother back, trying to make myself feel better, even if only for the moment. Leave it to my mother to set me straight and encourage me all at the same time. Angela didn't allow anyone to mistreat or talk bad about her daughter—not even her own daughter. I had to stop feeling sorry for myself and get back to business. Thankfully, I was starting a new job because everyone at my old office knew me as "Jeff and Kamryn," so we were usually invited to places as a couple. At least now, people would only know me as Kamryn, so I wouldn't have to repeat my breakup story a dozen times or get sympathy looks all day.

While my mom got started on a load of laundry, I headed upstairs to unpack some of my suitcases. My mother worked as a nurse in the ER for most of her life but eventually got tired of the chaotic schedule. She retired and started working part-time in a senior citizen home a few years back. She made sure to take the day off when I told her I was coming home. We decided to go out for lunch later to get some fresh air since the conversation earlier had made us both a little poignant.

My room hadn't changed much since I left for college, and I still had clothes in some of the drawers. I tried to sort through clothes that I could no longer wear, due to my "freshman fifteen" weight gain and the extra ten pounds I put on after that. I put a few clothes in the drawers, hung up some coats, set up my perfumes and lotions on my dresser, then decided to check my email. I plugged in my laptop, knowing the battery was about to die, and logged into my Gmail account. I immediately saw an email from Jeff and a few social media notifications from Instagram and Facebook. I ignored the email because I wasn't in the mood to hear from him so soon and decided to check Instagram first.

Jeff posted a picture of me as his "WCW"—Woman Crush Wednesday. Ironically, he hadn't posted pictures of me in years. He hardly ever posted pictures of us on his social media, and I tried not to ask. I wanted to believe that our relationship was deeper than a few Instagram and Facebook posts, so I rarely questioned him about it. Plus, I didn't make a habit of posting him, either, but that was different. I didn't want to look stupid in case some woman decided to reach out to me and claim to be sleeping with my boyfriend with the "I'm coming to you as a woman" speech.

The picture was from a double date that we went on two years ago with his boss, David Lancaster, and his wife, Jennifer. Jeff had landed a major contract with a new client that led to a quick promotion. Since Jeff and I rarely attended events together other than work, I jumped at the chance to go to dinner. Plus, Jennifer was nice, and we had become good friends over the last few years. Having significant others that were as career-focused as David and Jeff left room for many conversations for me and Jenny at galas, fundraisers, and charity events.

Jenny was an aspiring playwright with a lot of talent and vision. Luckily, being married to David gave Jenny a lot of time on her hands to focus on her craft. David seemed genuinely in love with his wife but uninterested in anything other than global investments. During dinner that night, I recalled her trying to interact with him to keep him involved in our conversation. But she and I ended up huddled in our own little world while the guys talked about market crashes, sports, and potential clients. That's the night Jenny told me how much she wanted children, but David had repeatedly declined. David and Jenny had a twenty-five-year age difference between the two of them. She had all these dreams of what her life would be like after marriage. Although she loved David, I could tell the loneliness of being married to a financial tycoon was starting to take its toll.

The waiter took a picture of us that night at Jeff's request, probably to savor the moment with his boss.

The second picture he posted was one he randomly took of me during a gala for his job. I don't know how he managed to take the picture in between texting people on his phone all night. I was chatting with some of his colleagues and glanced over at him, and I noticed he was pointing his phone at me. I walked over to him, asked what he was doing, and smiled slightly at the thought that he was admiring me for once. He leaned in close to me and told me how turned on he was watching me in my dress. He had been drinking a fair amount that night, but still, it was a compliment.

Thinking back to that very moment reminded me that our relationship wasn't all bad. But seconds after taking the picture, he was back on his phone responding to texts and emails. He told me the messages were all work-related, so I didn't make a fuss over it. Later that night when we were home, Jeff was in the shower, and I saw an "I miss you" text with the heart eyes emoji from an unsaved number in his phone. I questioned him, and he told me it was a coworker who kept pushing up on him at work and wouldn't take no for an answer. Always the liar.

I read the caption under the Instagram picture he posted of me:

"Best Friend and Love of My Life . . . Thank You for Always Being by My Side."

Just words. Was this public display of love and admiration supposed to win me over? He posted the same picture on Facebook and tagged me in it, as well. I quickly removed the tag and deleted the picture from my timeline. I thought about blocking him and changing my status, but that would cause too much unwanted attention. It didn't matter what it looked like on social media, anyway; I knew the truth, and soon, he would, too. It was over. No Facebook or Instagram post could change that. I clicked back to the email he sent and opened it.

Kamryn,

I miss you. I miss talking to you. This silent treatment every day is driving me crazy. I know I messed up. I know this is my fault, but I won't give up, Kamryn. I love you, and I don't want to lose you. I need you. Please talk to me so we can work this out. Hopefully, we can talk a little tonight when I get home. Love you. — J.R.

I contemplated responding to let him know that I wouldn't be there when he got home, and we had nothing else to talk about; to tell him that I was ready to move on with my life, and he should, too. But I didn't. I just closed the email and went back to unpacking. A few minutes later, my cell phone buzzed with a text message. Jeff, again. Damn. He was reaching out more today than he ever did before. I read the text:

I hope you're having a better day than me. I'm going crazy not speaking to you. Please don't give up on us.

I deleted the text to prevent myself from responding. I tossed the phone on the bed and kept unpacking. When I was finally able to unpack most of my things, I hopped in the shower to change before going to grab lunch with my mom. These past few weeks had been stressful, and I needed to refocus my energy on something other than my failed attempt at a relationship.

Lunch turned out to be a trip to the mall, dinner, and drinks. My mom dragged me into every store, saying, "Retail therapy always helps ease the pain after a breakup." She bought me a few dresses for work and a pair of shoes that she thought looked pretty on me, with the intention of borrowing them later, I'm sure. Then she insisted that I buy a body-con dress from Nordstrom that would be nearly impossible for me to fit my breasts into. The dress was simple and cute but was more for a body type that didn't require undergarments to keep things tucked and tight.

"Ma, where am I wearing this to? You know I can't fit my hips in this thing."

"Just try it on, Kamryn, please. Let's just see how it looks."

Tempted to roll my eyes, but smart enough not to, I walked over to the fitting room and obliged my mother's request. The dress stretched more than I thought it would and surprisingly hugged my curves without my span. I stepped out to find my mother still occupied browsing for sexy dresses.

"Mom, look. I guess it fits okay. It just needs a blazer to cover my arms, right?"

"*Okay*? Kamryn, this dress is more than okay. It fits perfectly, and you look amazing in it. And if you try to put a blazer over it, I'll burn it."

"Fine, Mom. I'll get it. But that's it."

"Great! They also have it in blue. I'll meet you at the counter." Angela dashed back into the aisle and got lost in a sea of dresses, apparently not acknowledging my "that's it" statement.

Back at the house, I hurried upstairs to kick off my shoes and loosen my bra. I forgot how draining and tiring shopping can be. My mother was still busying herself around the house, completely unfazed by four hours of mall shopping.

I had my phone off for most of the afternoon to avoid getting phone calls or texts from Jeff while we were out. When I finally turned my phone on, I had thirteen texts and four calls from him alone. And one missed call and text from Mica.

The first few texts from Jeff were him just asking where I went and what time I was coming back home. The texts started to escalate once he realized my things were gone. According to the exclamation points and capitalization of his words, he seemed terribly upset that I moved my things out of the house without notice. Then, the texts became more urgent, with him repeatedly asking where I was and where my things were and pleading for me to come home. I couldn't help but smirk at his frustration. It probably wasn't right to leave him high and dry, but Jeff had put me through hell over the years. Maybe now, he would understand what I felt when he abandoned me all those nights. I turned my phone back off without responding to any of his texts and got ready for bed.

CHAPTER 5
Mr. Pop-up

The next few days, I focused on organizing my room, moving some of my things into a small storage space, and looking through a few work emails. I'd promised Mr. Harold that I would close out any outstanding projects while I was on vacation for the last week. Luckily, I didn't have much to do since Ted stepped up and took over. I started looking more into Alpine Bloom and digging up whatever I could find on the previous director. From what I could tell—via social media, of course—the previous director retired and moved to the Caribbean. Unfortunately, there was no information on the director who held the position right before me for four months. After looking over all their publications and media deals that I could find online, I had a better understanding of Alpine Bloom's marketing style but no real clue about what direction they wanted to head towards next.

By Saturday, I knew I could no longer avoid Jeff. He had been calling and texting all week. He finally called my mother's house looking for me early in the morning, and that was a big mistake. Angela didn't lie to him, but she also didn't tell him I was there at the time. However, she did let him have an earful. She tried to remain quiet, but Jeff's pleas only frustrated her. I guess I should have taken the phone to relieve Jeff from my mother's onslaught, but my mom had disconnected the call before I could interject. On purpose, of course. Now, today was no different; Jeff was texting me, asking if I was okay and if we could talk. That was two hours ago. I finally gave in and responded.

Kamryn: I'm fine, Jeff. I'm staying with my mom for a little while. You can stop calling.

Jeff: Kamryn, it's been a week! Why did you leave? We need to talk about this. I need to see you. Now!

Kamryn: No, we don't. Seeing you and talking is not an option.

Jeff: Baby . . . pls don't do this. Pls don't leave me, Kamryn. Just talk to me, pls . . . I can explain.

I felt my anger rising every time he thought he could just "explain" himself out of a lie. I didn't want to argue; I just wanted this to be over. Arguing would only make matters worse because I would have to keep reliving the hurt and listening to his nonsense, and we were past that.

Kamryn: I'm not interested in your explanation on how you got another woman pregnant . . . again! I don't care anymore . . . I'm done.

Jeff didn't respond after that. Maybe he had finally got the picture, which made me feel relieved. The constant phone calls and texts were starting to wear me out. Once, I almost gave in and agreed to see him—not because I was interested in hearing what he had to say but mainly to see how I would respond to seeing him. How would I feel? Would I attack him? Curse him out? Or just ignore him? It didn't matter now.

I decided to go for a run to relieve some tension. I grabbed my cell phone and threw on a hoodie to fight some of the early morning chill. I headed outside and jogged toward the park across the street from my mom's house. There's a small track inside, but it gets boring after a while, so I decided to take the city streets. Jogging through the park near our old townhouse—Jeff's townhouse, not ours—was always relaxing to me. But today, I felt a little distracted. Instead of enjoying the scenery, I was looking at all the people, families in particular. Everywhere I glanced, there was a mother playing with her kids, fathers pushing their kids on the swing or catching them from the bottom of the slide. I saw couples jogging together, walking together, sitting together, or just laughing together. *Together*. Everywhere I looked, I saw people together. I'd never felt so empty until this very moment. How had I gone from being in love, engaged, and planning a future to this?

I thought back to when Jeff had proposed. We were home, and I had been giving Jeff the cold shoulder for a few days. I had confronted him about being a little too friendly with a coworker. He had been in a car accident earlier that week, and, thankfully, he wasn't hurt, just a minor fender bender. I remember being so concerned for him, catering to him like a mother does a child when he came home from the accident. Soon after, the insurance company called to get additional information on the passenger. Jeff wasn't home, so I told the insurance representative that Jeff was the only person in the car, since that's what Jeff told me. The woman corrected me again and said the police report had two names listed: Jeffrey Rose and Tiffany Miller. I hung up the phone and called Jeff's assistant.

****

"Good afternoon. Jeffrey Rose's office. How may I help you?"

"Hi, Tiffany. It's Kamryn."

"Oh! Hi, Ms. Hanover. Hold one moment, and I'll see if he's available for you."

"No, that's okay. I actually called to speak to you."

"Oh." She paused. "How can I help you?"

"Did you happen to leave your sunglasses in Jeff's car last week? I found a pair, and they're not mine, so I figured I'd ask you," I lied.

I wanted to see if she would admit to being in his car—or, even better, sleeping with him. Tiffany remained silent on the phone. I imagined her sitting there looking nervous, trying to figure out what to say next.

"Uhhh . . . I . . . I don't know." She was so flustered that she couldn't even control her stammer.

"You don't know if they are your sunglasses or if you were in Jeff's car?"

"Umm . . . No, ma'am. I've never been in Mr. Rose's car," she lied.

"Well, I figured they might be yours since you and Jeff are so . . . close." Another lifeline extended.

"No, they're not mine, Ms. Hanover."

"Humph, that's strange. I wonder whose they could be, then."

"I don't know. I'm sorry." Of course, she didn't know I was lying.

Tiffany was young and easily impressionable. I could tell from the few times we met that she was easily mesmerized by Jeff. He probably fed her some story about not being happy with me and wanting to start over with her, and she believed him. We all did. I wonder how she felt now, thinking that Jeff may have another "other" woman.

"I'm sure you are. Thanks for your help, Tiffany." This little witch really thought she was clever.

"No problem, Ms. Hanover. Have a great—"

"Oh, Tiffany, I almost forgot. Our insurance company called. They wanted to confirm your insurance information and know if you were seeking medical treatment."

"Excuse me?" She sounded confused.

"You know, from the car accident the other day. You must have been in Jeff's car, then, right?"

The phone went completely silent. All I could hear was Tiffany's breathing through the receiver.

"Hello?"

"Yes . . . I'm sorry. I didn't . . . umm . . ." There she was, stammering her words again.

"It's okay, Tiffany. I trust that you'll keep this little conversation between us, correct?"

"Yes, ma'am."

"Good." I ended the call. Hopefully, she was just as embarrassed and mad as I was.

When he came home, I casually asked Jeff about the details surrounding the accident, telling him I had to clear up a few things for the insurance company. I asked him if he was by himself, and he, being the liar that he was, said yes. That was the start of another argument until Jeff confessed and told me he was just giving Tiffany a ride home. He only lied because he knew I would overreact. After I threatened to leave, he admitted to me that Tiffany had come on to him a few times, but he turned her down. That was also a lie.

A few days after that, Jeff came home with a ring and asked me to marry him over dinner. I hesitated, but in the end, I said yes. The "yes" that came from my lips didn't silence the "no" that was screaming in my head. I chose to ignore it and move forward with love. Now, looking at the people on the street, I wondered if Jeff and I ever had that. Were we ever really in love? Maybe back in college or when we first graduated, but that was so long ago. How had these people managed to make it work and be so happy? In seven years, I hadn't figured out how to make my relationship work. I hadn't mastered how to get him not to cheat. I cooked, I cleaned, I worked, I was educated, I loved, I supported, I encouraged, and, most importantly, I forgave. It wasn't like sex was an issue. Although the sex wasn't always the best, we still managed to make it work. So, how did these people make it work? What did these women have that I didn't? Why was everyone so happy during my time of despair? It felt as though the world was in love, and I was alone and broken. Looking at the people in the park made me miss Jeff. We shared so much together—so many laughs, memories, and experiences that I couldn't easily replace.

But I couldn't continue to forgive and love someone who didn't respect me. I wouldn't do it anymore.

I started to feel a light burn in my legs and glanced at my watch. I had been jogging and walking for nearly forty minutes. I picked up the pace and decided to head back home. Twenty minutes later, I made a left on Story Avenue and jogged to the street vendor to grab a bottle of water. I was about ten minutes away from my mother's house and decided to walk the rest of the way. I took my phone out of my arm band and checked my messages. About fifteen messages from the group chat: Mica, Nicole, Natalie, and Lauren. They were giving suggestions about plans for tonight. Clubs, movies, lounges, and malls were all the places I didn't want to go, so I decided to ignore the messages until I had a better excuse for not being able to go.

I turned the corner to my mother's block, chugging the rest of my water, and immediately stopped when I saw him. I saw his car first, parked right out front. Then, I saw him leaning on the steps of my mother's front porch. He saw me approaching and stood straight up, waiting for me to reach him. I realized that I had stopped walking and tried to regain my composure. I straightened my posture to make sure I still had my spine in tack before I continued to walk toward the house. When I was about five feet away, I stopped and looked him square in the eyes. He made a move to hug me like we were old friends, so I folded my arms in front of my chest and took another step back.

"I see you're making surprise visits today."

"I had to see you. And you're not answering my calls. What else am I supposed to do?"

"Okay. You've seen me; now, you can leave." I started to walk by him, but Jeff moved to block me. I stopped walking only to avoid touching him.

"Kamryn, why are you doing this? Why can't you just talk to me?" Jeff pleaded.

"Why am *I* doing this? Seriously, just leave. Because you standing here asking me a dumb ass question is just going to piss me off."

"Baby, look. I know I fucked up, okay? I know that. All I'm asking is if we can talk. I want to talk to you so we can start to work this out."

"Work what out, exactly?"

"Us," Jeff responded somberly.

"Us? Why do I have to work on *us* because *you* fucked up? You always fuck up. This is what you do, Jeff. You cheat because you are a cheater. You lie because you are a liar. And then, you come begging me to work shit out. Why, Jeff? Why do *I* have to keep working things out because *you* keep fucking us up?"

Jeff stood there in silence for a moment, glancing at me as if he didn't recognize the woman standing in front of him. Admittedly, I almost didn't recognize her, either. It had been a while since I spoke up and avoided falling into his arms. It was a surprise to see him at a loss for words. In all the years and all the arguments, I had done most of the crying and very little fighting.

Jeff pleaded. "Kamryn . . . why are you speak—"

"Jeff, you should leave. I'm done with this conversation. I left your ring on the table, so you should have everything you need from me."

"Yeah, you left your ring and a note. Don't I deserve more than that? Kamryn, none of those other women meant anything to me. None of them mattered. All I want is you. I'm sorry. Please come home with me." He actually looked sad, and I almost felt sorry for him.

"I am home, Jeff. I'm not leaving with you, so you wasted your time coming here. Bye."

I moved past Jeff and hurried up the steps towards the front door. Jeff turned to go after me and reached for my arm. When I felt him touch me, I yanked my arm away hard enough to startle him.

"Kamryn! What the hell?! We're supposed to be getting married. You have to at least talk to me."

"Married? Are you completely clueless, Jeff?"

"No, I'm hopeful and begging for you to at least talk to me. If you still love me, why can't we just talk?"

Jeff reached out to grab my hand and pulled me in close to him. It was a gesture I had become all too familiar with: the hand touches and quick embrace, with a subtle kiss to my cheek. I played each step in my memory as he stood in front of me.

"Because love just isn't enough, Jeff. Not right now."

"If not now, then when, Kamryn? Just tell me when you're ready to talk to me, and I'll be there, so we can work this out."

I released my hands from his grip and walked in the house, closing the door. I ran upstairs to my room and looked through the window to see if he was still there. He was walking back to his car now, holding his phone. *Humph. Probably texting another woman.* I tossed my phone on the bed, took off my sweaty clothes, and threw them into the hamper. Standing in the shower, I felt proud of myself for standing up to Jeff face-to-face without tears. It had been so long since I felt good about a decision I made concerning him. This finally felt right.

After I got dressed, I headed into the hall to look for my mother. Surprisingly, she hadn't come out of the house when Jeff was there. I knew she was home because her car was still parked in the driveway. I found her sitting in her room drinking a cup of hot tea.

"Hey, Mom."

"Hey, sweetie," Angela said with a smile, peering over her cup of tea.

"I guess you missed the little show out front, huh?" I asked.

"Missed it?" Angela chuckled. "I got a front row seat. The picture and audio were great from where I was."

"Yeah, I'm sure we put on a show. It's just so frustrating."

"What is?" Angela asked.

"He is. Standing there looking all sad and sorry, like I'm supposed to forgive him again and pretend like nothing ever happened. You know, he actually expected me to just get in the car and go with him."

"I heard." Angela looked at me while I vented.

"I can't believe him. He expects me to just walk back into this mess he created. I'm not doing it."

When I appeared to be done, Angela put her cup down on the nightstand and looked at me.

"You know, it's natural to be frustrated. It'll probably be a while until you're not frustrated with him and this whole situation.

I can tell you that it does get better with time—not because you'll forget, but because eventually, other things will take the place of what you're worried about now. And one day, you may wake up and be reminded of him and get mad all over again. It won't be as bad as it is now, but it may still sting a little. And that's okay, too. Just know that things will get better, and you making the decision to love and respect yourself is never the wrong decision."

"Thanks, Mom."

"Now, let me go run to the store to get a few things. Be back in jiff."

CHAPTER 6
Mr. Fine as Hell

I called Mica as soon as I went back to my room. It was time to stop living like a wounded animal. Why should I stay cooped up in the house? I still hadn't responded to the group earlier. After 137 messages, they decided we were meeting at Club NOVA later that night. I rarely had the chance to go out with the girls like I used to. Between work, grad school, and living a little further away, I was usually busy with something else. I dialed Mica, and, as usual, she answered on the first ring.

"It's about time! We've been texting you all morning. Where have you been?"

"Yeah, I saw all the texts; that's why I'm calling. I went for a run, and then I ran into Jeff."

"Jeff? Where?!" Mica asked.

"In front of my mom's house. He just showed up here, asking me to come home."

"Are you serious? Oh, my God! Did Ms. Angie beat him with her broom?" Mica chuckled into the phone.

"No, she spared him his life this time."

"Humph. Lucky for him."

"Yeah. I will tell you about it later. So, who's going to Club NOVA tonight?"

"So far, just me, you, Nic, Lauren, Drew, and Charlie. Charlie said Ryan might swing by on his way back from his trip. A few of my colleagues will be there, too, but they'll be at a separate table."

"What time is everyone getting there?"

"Be there by 10:00 p.m. Make sure you're sexy, cute, and revealing. It's a celebration!"

I rolled my eyes at Mica's request for my attire. "Okay. Bye!"

"Don't roll your eyes at me! Bye, girl!" Mica laughed as she hung up the phone.

I hadn't been out in a while, so who knows if what I had in my closet was considered sexy anymore. I definitely needed to wear black to help camouflage my tummy, and today was my first decent workout in weeks, so I needed all the help I could get. I ruffled through the closet and pulled out a couple of old dresses, some of which I hadn't worn in years: a black sweater dress that covered up the girls in the front and a fitted dress with ruching on the sides to help conceal the hips with a deep V-neckline.

After going through my entire wardrobe and taking a break, I still didn't have a clue. I heard my mom's key at the front door and rushed down the stairs to meet her.

"Hey, Mom."

"Oh, hi, sweetie. You startled me."

"Sorry. I need your help."

"What's wrong?" She immediately looked concerned.

"Oh, nothing. I think I might go out tonight, and I need help finding something to wear. Nothing I have works."

Angela stopped and turned to face me. "I think that's a good idea." She was smiling now. "It's good to get out of the house sometimes."

"Yeah. I spoke to Michelle, and we're going to meet up later with Nicole and Lauren."

"Oh, good. How's she doing?"

"She's good. Still sharing the same contempt for Jeff as you do." I smiled at her.

"Glad to know I'm not alone. Where are you ladies going?"

"Club NOVA."

"Do you know what color you're going to wear?" I know my mom was trying her hardest not to sound too pushy or nosy.

"Black. I was trying to decide which dress to wear before you came home." I then remembered that I hadn't decided on a pair of shoes or accessories to go with my dress. "I was told to be sexy, cute and revealing."

"Oh, goody!" Angela squealed while clapping her hands together. "We get to play dress-up!"

My mother has always had a keen sense of fashion and style. She always knew what would look good on her. Although very meticulous, her style was effortless. She rushed upstairs into my bedroom and saw the selection of dresses thrown across the bed. I walked in behind her and leaned on the dresser to watch her work.

"See my dilemma?" I spoke.

"Oh, no, darling. I see opportunity. This dress will be perfect with the right bra," she said, holding up the V-neck dress. "You just go and fix yourself something to eat. I'll work out the details here."

Later that evening, I was standing in front of the mirror, amazed at how good I looked. I was beginning to think I was a little too fancy, and then recalled a few of Mica's colleagues. They all dressed nice and looked more like fashion models than teachers. Not that I didn't consider myself stylish, but I was a bit more conservative.

I rubbed my hands down my dress, over my waist and my hips. The dress hugged my curves perfectly. My waist appeared smaller with the ruching on the side—or was it just that my hips looked bigger? Either way, I looked good, and I felt sexy. These spanx didn't hurt, either; like I said, I needed all the help I could get. My double D breasts sat perfectly at the top of the dress like melons. I turned in the mirror to get a look at my butt; not too shabby. The black strappy sandals and gold accessories my mom picked out made the look come together. I did my hair in soft curls that fell to my shoulders, with minimal makeup, black eyeliner, mascara, and a red lip.

I decided not to drive since I knew I would be drinking with Nicole's crazy self. She was my ultimate drinking partner in college. I glanced at the cable box in my room. Shoot. 10:04 p.m. I'd been getting ready all day and still somehow managed to be late. I requested an Uber, grabbed my clutch and my leather jacket, and headed downstairs.

Walking into NOVA at 10:40 p.m., I immediately knew I wasn't overdressed. The crowd looked like something out of a fashion magazine. Everyone had on the latest designer shoes and handbags. Even the men looked out of my league. I scooted through the crowd after getting through security. I texted the group chat to let them know I was there, but wasn't sure if anyone would hear their phone over the loud music. I peeked over the crowd as much as I could in my heels. Even with my height, the crowd of people made it difficult to look around.

"Kamryn!"

Thankfully, I heard Mica's voice. I turned to see her waving at me. Mica pushed through the crowd with ease, probably because she was used to this type of chaos.

"Oh, my God, Kamryn! You look amazing! Where have you been hiding that body?!" Mica hugged me and gushed over my outfit.

"Oh, hush. It's been here. Just been in the house for a while."

"Well, you look amazing."

"Thanks, sis. This place is kind of crowded, huh?"

"This? Oh, please. The crowd hasn't even begun yet. Come on; we're over here."

Mica grabbed my hand and pulled me to a back area, where the music wasn't as loud. I saw a table with food, bottles of premium liquor, and drinks on it. Exactly like I thought—fancy. Looking around the table, I saw Nicole; Mica's boyfriend, Charlie; and Ryan. Ryan Ellis was Charlie's best friend practically since birth. They grew up together, went to the same college, and somehow ended up living in the same area after school. Charlie was a teacher, like Mica, and ran an after-school recreational center. Ryan was a businessman—at least that's what I called him because I had no clue what he did besides work out at the gym. I noticed him just standing there, trying to blend in with the crowd. But he was too handsome to blend and annoying as hell. He had all the right features: tall, dreamy eyes, charming smile, and a body made in heaven. His arms were the size of boulders, and his chest muscles appeared subtly under every shirt he wore.

******

"Kamryn!" Nicole screamed. "OMG! You look amazing!"

"I know, right?! That's what I told her," Mica added. I laughed at the sight of my two friends gushing over me.

"Hey, Nic! You look great as usual," I said as I hugged her.

"Kamryn?" Charlie asked. "Hey! I thought that was you. How are ya?"

"Hey, Charlie. I'm good; can't complain."

As I gave Charlie a hug, I caught a glance of that stunning face standing behind him. When Charlie stepped to the side, there he was, almost as if he was waiting to greet me. I could feel his eyes gazing up and down my body. Was he really checking me out? Having his eyes on me suddenly made me feel insecure. I started to tug at my dress, pulling it down, and placed a hand on my stomach. This awkward stare down he was giving me felt like it lasted for ten minutes, when it may have only been a few seconds.

"Look what the cat dragged in," Ryan stated.

Back to reality. Hearing Ryan's voice reminded me of how obnoxious he was. He was always a man of few words, but when we did speak, he was guaranteed to say something to get under my skin.

"Hey, Ryan," I stated flatly.

"Hello, Kamryn," Ryan responded.

I leaned in and gave him a friendly hug, taking in his scent. I think I closed my eyes and breathed a little too hard when I hugged him. He smelled like fresh Irish Spring soap and expensive cologne. As Charlie's best friend, Ryan was always around and usually at Mica's functions. We've exchanged a few words over the years, but nothing more than the usual snide remarks. I had the funny feeling that Ryan wasn't too fond of Jeff, which perhaps is why he kept his distance.

"It's good to see you." He looked me up and down again.

"Good to see you too, Ryan." Lord, have mercy. This man was gorgeous. Breathe, Kamryn, breathe.

"Come on! Let's get some drinks!" Mica yelled over the music.

" Drinks? There's plenty . . ." Charlie started to say.

Before he could finish his obvious statement, Mica pulled me back through the crowd, leading straight to the bar. Even with a hundred people leaning over the bar, Mica maneuvered her way into the space. She placed an order for a ginger ale and a bottle of water while I kept my fingers busy with my hair.

"Thanks for the diversion."

"Sure. Stop messing with your hair, girl, before you mess it up. It looks great!" Mica yelled over the music.

The bartender came back with the drinks, and Mica handed me the ginger ale. She knew me too well. I used to drink ginger ale in college at parties anytime I didn't want to get too drunk. It was the closest thing to a mixed drink that I enjoyed. Mica preferred a Coca-Cola or Pepsi.

"So, Lauren didn't get here yet?" I asked, leaning into her.

"No, she said she couldn't make it. A stomach bug or something like that."

"Hmm." That's all I could say as I looked around the club, trying not to glance in the direction towards the table.

"Do you think it'll be weird between you two after the breakup?"

"No, it shouldn't be. She could barely tolerate her brother, so if anything, she would understand."

I didn't sound too convincing to myself, so I knew Mica wasn't buying it. I hadn't thought about how the breakup would affect my friendship with Lauren. Even though she had suggested I break up with Jeff dozens of times before, it was always as a joke. Admittedly, I was a little nervous about seeing her tonight. At least one of us had the sense to back out.

"Well, I hope not. One has nothing to do with the other. If anything, she should be helping you key his car."

I chuckled at my friend's hint of violence and glanced over at the table. Damn. He's looking at me, and we made eye contact. I quickly tried to avert my gaze somewhere else, but I felt Mica's eyes on me.

"What?" I asked.

"Don't 'What?' me like I didn't just catch the googly eyes between you and Mr. Ellis. He's been staring at you since we walked over here. So obvious about it, too."

"So?"

"*So?* So, what are you going to do about it?" Mica was starting to interrogate me.

"Absolutely nothing. I don't want anything to do with him. Or anyone else, for that matter."

"So, you're just going to avoid all men now?"

"Hmm, pretty much."

"Hey, are y'all done gossiping over here? Because I know you're not getting drinks." Nicole popped up next to us.

"No. I'm about to learn why Kamryn is giving up on all men," Mica responded.

"I just got out of a relationship; I don't need to jump back into one."

"No, but you do need to jump *on* something." Nic added her perverted two cents as usual, and they both laughed.

"Y'all are sick, and the both of you need Jesus."

"Kamryn, Jeff was one bad asshole. I mean, you wasted a few years. But don't end your sex life because of it," Mica stated.

"Sex life? I need to get my entire life together, not just the sex part. Besides, sex is not really an issue."

"Wait, so you and Jeff are still doing it?!" Nic nearly screamed over the music.

"No, girl. Hush! We are not doing it! We haven't done it since I found out, but we were doing it regularly before. So, I figure I won't need any service for at least a couple of months. Plus, sex complicates things. And I don't need any distractions right now."

"Hmm, okay. We'll see about that. Cause from the look of things, you might be getting distracted and *serviced* a little sooner than you think." Mica sipped her water and diverted her eyes back to the table.

Both Charlie and Ryan were looking in our direction. Charlie was waving his hands at Mica, gesturing for her to come back. The cuteness almost made me sick. I glanced at Ryan and caught him gazing at my body again. I inadvertently placed my hand over my belly, causing Ryan to look at my face. We locked eyes for a moment—no smiles. His gaze made me feel like I was under a spotlight. I broke the connection by pretending to be interested in something on the dance floor.

"Girl, please. We can barely stand each other. He's not my type, anyway."

Nic almost choked on her water. "And what type is that?! The fine as hell type?!" She caught on to conversation quickly.

"He's all right."

"Yeah, okay. Come on, girl. Let's go back before Charlie's hands fall off. Isn't he so cute?"

"Yeah, girl." I whispered to myself, "He is fine as hell," still talking about Ryan.

They walked over to the table and made themselves a drink. Mica asked a passing security worker to take a group picture of all of us. He took it without giving us a countdown, and we all looked unready; cute but not ready. Nicole asked a woman standing close enough to our area if she could take a cute picture in exchange for a free drink. The girl agreed and put her almost empty drink and clutch down on our table, obviously up for the challenge. She took several pictures and choreographed each of our positions, obviously a professional. One of the pictures resulted in Ryan standing right next to me, with his arm around my waist at the direction of our photographer. I think he held me tighter than necessary, causing our bodies to lean into one another. Mica whispered "Sookie, Sookie, now," in my ear, causing me to laugh right as the woman snapped the picture.

When it was finally done, I hurried back to my seat at the table on the opposite end of Ryan. Feeling his hands on my body nearly sent vibrations through my spine. The smell of his cologne was still lingering in my nostrils from standing so close, and it was almost too much to bear. If I were lucky, his scent would still be there when I got home.

CHAPTER 7
Goddess Special

Ryan was thankful for the distraction that Michelle created. Maybe she noticed the tension between Kamryn and him. As soon as he touched her, he had this uncontrollable urge to kiss her in front of everyone. And he thought he just might have, until Michelle snatched her away. What the hell was wrong with him? Kamryn was off limits and somewhat unattainable. But that didn't stop him from staring at her over by the bar. She caught him twice, but that wasn't enough to make him stop. Now, as they all made their way around the table into the booth, Ryan found himself sitting directly across from Kamryn. As the drinks were flowing, Ryan listened to everyone talk most of the night, laughing at some of Drew's stories about some chick he was dating and watching the women take selfies all night. But he was completely distracted with her there. He had never seen her look this way before, and it was starting to mess with his brain.

He watched Kamryn across from him for most of the night. He couldn't take his eyes off her. Kamryn was always beautiful, but tonight, she looked like a goddess. When he first saw her walking towards the table with Michelle, he couldn't believe his eyes. Watching her smile while she greeted her friends made the room move in slow motion. When it was his turn to speak, he didn't know what to say. As usual, he said the first thing that came out of his mouth. Not "hello," "hi," or "nice to see you again." No—he had said the dumbest thing ever: "Look what the cat dragged in." Who says that? Mostly idiots. His brain stopped working, and his mouth froze. When she hugged him, he smelled her perfume and had to suppress a low groan. Just looking at her from across the table now heightened every nerve in his body.

She was gorgeous. Her body looked marvelous in that black dress, as if it was painted over every curve of her body. He noticed her trying to cover up her stomach with her hand, and he couldn't figure out why. Maybe she was having cramps or something. He loved Kamryn's curves and all her thickness. He imagined how soft her body would feel next to his. Looking at her now, he knew he wanted her badly. Her full breasts, thick thighs, and plump lips were all screaming for attention tonight, and he knew he was just the man to give it to her.

Just then, as he was deep in thought about her, she threw her head back and laughed, exposing more of her neck. He started daydreaming again about kissing her all over. Unexpectedly, he felt himself growing beneath the table and immediately deterred his thoughts back to the conversation.

"Kamryn, how's the new job going? Mica told me you switched companies," Charlie asked.

"I start on Monday. I'm looking forward to finally working in marketing. Just hoping I can keep up."

"That's awesome! Congrats!" Charlie yelled over the music.

"Baby, come dance with me! I love this song!" Michelle said as she scooted out of the booth towards the dance floor.

"Right behind you, babe," Charlie said as he grabbed Michelle's hand and followed behind her.

Nicole had already found herself a warm body to dance next to while Drew was cuddled in a corner talking to a new playmate, so that left Kamryn at the table alone with him. Ryan noticed Kamryn move in her seat and shift her gaze away from him. Maybe in an effort to avoid me, due to that stupid comment I made earlier, he thought. He barely made any effort to speak with her all night, so maybe he was avoiding her, too.

"It's nice to see you again." Ryan tried to project his voice over the music.

"Yeah, I think you said that already. Nice to see you, too." Kamryn gave a subtle smirk. He always admired her sarcasm.

"Congrats on the new job. I didn't realize you were looking to leave the old one."

"Yeah, it was time to go. It wasn't aligned with my career goals." Kamryn held his attention as she spoke, staring directly at him. He almost forgot to talk back.

After a long pause, Ryan said, "That's good. Really clever."

"How about you? How are things?" Kamryn asked.

"Things are good. I can't complain." Ryan rarely talked about business or his company amongst friends. So, he really didn't know how else to answer the question.

"That's good. How was your vacation?" Kamryn responded.

"My vacation?" Ryan pondered the question with a raised brow.

"Oh, Michelle mentioned you just got back from a trip. I assumed it was a vacation."

"Oh, no. It was a business trip."

"Oh okay. Good trip?"

"Yeah, great."

Why was he finding it so difficult to have a conversation with her? He had spoken to her dozens of times over the years, and now, all of a sudden, he couldn't strike up a single decent conversation. Ryan caught himself staring at her breasts twice. Once, he even started licking his lips and wishing he were kissing her nipples. He needed to stay focused. Kamryn had a boyfriend,

Jeff. He couldn't stand the guy, but she was still taken. And Ryan made it his business to respect relationships.

By the end of the night, everyone started to say their goodbyes standing outside of Club NOVA. Ryan was standing next to Kamryn and could smell her perfume. At this angle, he could see directly down her dress into her full breasts every time he looked down at her. Not that he was trying to look; he just couldn't help that he was six-foot-four and they were in his immediate line of vision. It wasn't as if he was blind.

"Kamryn, do you want to stay over at my place tonight? Charlie can drop us off," Michelle asked.

"No, that's okay. I have to get up early for church. I'll take an Uber."

Ryan wanted to offer her a ride, but he didn't want to come off too eager. He averted his gaze away from her to prevent another accidental growth. She has a boyfriend, remember? Simmer down, boy; simmer down.

"How far is it?" Michelle chimed in.

Kamryn took a moment to check her phone, and then sucked her teeth. "Damn it. They canceled."

"I can take you," Ryan blurted out a little too abruptly, causing a couple of eyes to dart his way.

"That's okay; I'll get another one. Thanks," she replied while swiftly typing into her phone.

"At this time, it may take forever. Just stay over at my place," Michelle insisted.

"I really don't mind." Ryan made another attempt, thankfully less eager this time.

"C'mon, Kamryn. Let the guy be a gentleman. You hung out with us tonight, so it's only right that someone takes you home. Besides, Michelle will be busy tonight," Charlie interjected, causing Michelle to chuckle and smile at him affectionately.

Kamryn

Watching these two flirts almost made Kamryn gag, but she loved to see them together. Mica was a free spirit who loved to be in love, despite getting hurt in her last relationship. After Mica's last boyfriend in college, "Blake the Snake," she swore off men. She focused on doing what she loved most, teaching, and she was great at it. She met Charlie while on a retreat with some of her colleagues a few years ago. Charlie was speaking at the same retreat, and once they locked eyes, they had been inseparable ever since. Charlie was sweet and the true definition of a gentleman, which is more than she could say for his best buddy, Ryan.

"So, is that a, yes?" Ryan asked, giving her an intense look.

All eyes now on her, Kamryn felt it would be too weird to continue to object. It's just a ride home, right? No big deal. It hardly mattered that she caught him looking at her several times tonight and couldn't keep her thoughts off of him. She felt like a specimen under his peering eyes and extremely uncomfortable.

"Okay, sure. Thank you," Kamryn finally responded.

"Ryan, take care of my friend." Mica gave him a threatening look as she reached over to hug Kamryn goodnight. "I can and will kill you. You know that, don't you?"

"She means it," Charlie added as he pulled Mica towards him.

"I'll text you when I get home," Kamryn said.

"Okay. Talk to you tomorrow," Nicole added as she walked toward the parking lot with Charlie and Mica.

"I'm parked over here," Ryan said as they headed towards the street.

Ryan placed a hand on Kamryn's back and guided her towards his car. Kamryn focused on her breathing to distract herself from his touch. Once they were at his car, Ryan walked her to the passenger side and opened the door, again placing his hand on her back.

"I guess I'm getting the full service tonight, huh?" she said nervously.

"It's the goddess special. Comes with door-to-door service and good conversation," Ryan responded.

"Is that so?" Kamryn said with a smirk and rolled her eyes.

In the few years she'd known Ryan, he never said anything remotely nice to her. Only cynical comments that continually proved he was a bit of a jackass. She slid in the car and relaxed into the soft leather. He closed her door gently, then walked over to the driver's side and got in.

"Are you comfortable?" Ryan asked.

"Yes. Thank you."

"You still live near Westchester Square, right?" Ryan asked.

"Good memory, but no. I'm back in Greensburg."

"Oh, I didn't realize you moved."

"You were going to take me all the way to Westchester Square? Do you realize how far that is?" Kamryn asked.

"It's not too far. It's late, and there's no traffic," Ryan explained.

"It's too far for you to randomly be taking me home."

"Goddess service," he reminded her.

While Kamryn put the address into his navigation system, Ryan started the car and pulled away from the curb.

"So, how are you and Jeff enjoying the suburbs?" Ryan inquired, attempting to appear nonchalant.

Kamryn paused. Questions about Jeff made her uncomfortable. She'd been avoiding them all night.

"It's okay."

"I'm surprised he'd ever leave the Square, considering how much he talked about it."

Kamryn took a deep breath. Here goes.

"He didn't. We broke up."

"Oh, wow. I'm sorry to hear that." He lied. Granted, he was surprised to hear her say that.

"Don't be. It was for the best."

Ryan looked over at her. Her words seemed joyful, but her voice was dejected.

"Are you okay?" he asked.

Shocked by his question, she looked at him. "Yeah, I'm fine." The last thing she wanted to do was discuss her ex, especially with Ryan. She recalled Ryan flaunting around a few models last year at Charlie's birthday party and figured that was a better conversation, so she quickly attempted to change the subject.

"What about you?" she asked.

"What about me?"

"Are you still trying to date all the Victoria's Secret models?" she asked in a tone that was more accusatory than inquisitive.

Most likely stunned by her question, Ryan paused slightly before answering.

"As I recall, I only dated one Victoria's Secret model. And I didn't know you were paying attention to who I dated."

"How could I not? She sashayed around Charlie's party like it was a runway the entire time." She heard Ryan let out a low chuckle and tried to control her hormones. "You two looked good together, though."

"No, we didn't. Don't lie. I didn't invite her that day; she just showed up. I try not to mix my business with pleasure."

"Business with pleasure, huh? So, was your Victoria's Secret date just pleasure or all business?" Kamryn inquired.

Ryan paused and looked straight at the road, unsure of how to respond.

"It was complicated."

"Don't worry about it. Forget I asked. It's really none of my business what your business or pleasure is." Kamryn mumbled the last part. She was curious but not enough to hear about Ryan's sexual exploits with his dates.

"It was business for her. And I cut her off once I realized that," Ryan responded.

Ryan

Ryan thought back to the night Claudia showed up to Charlie's party. She was too much of a drama queen, and he was thankful that he noticed that after a few months. Claudia showed up that night as a ploy to get him back and practically embarrassed him with her antics, although no one could probably tell. He was thoroughly aggravated the whole night and tried his best to keep his cool.

"She was the only model, though. I'm not that superficial." He tried to break the silence.

"I didn't mean to imply that. It's really none of my business. Just noticed you have a type; that's all."

"Oh, I do? What type is that?" Ryan's attention was piqued.

"The Victoria's Secret type," Kamryn answered with a smirk.

Oh, how she couldn't be further from the truth, Ryan thought. But he decided not to correct her tonight. "And what's your type?" Ryan asked while looking at her and trying to focus on the road, which was becoming a very difficult task.

Kamryn turned to look him directly in his eyes when she answered, making Ryan's blood rush to one spot in his body all at once.

"The loyal, faithful, and honest type." She stared at him with so much intensity when their eyes locked that he almost forgot he was driving. Her face was so beautiful. If he could, he would've leaned over and kissed her right then and there.

"So, why didn't you and your ex work out? You two seemed happy." Ryan lied again. She never seemed happy with him. Charlie and Michelle were happy. Kamryn just seemed content.

Ryan waited for her to answer while looking away and pretending to check his mirrors for other cars. What he was really doing was trying to calm his loins and not kiss Kamryn in his car. Her perfume was starting to overwhelm his senses, so he cracked the window to get some fresh air.

Kamryn

"It turns out he wasn't my type." Kamryn sighed and stared out the window, breathing in the fresh air.

They were getting close to her house, so she started digging in her purse for her keys. Ryan stayed quiet for the rest of the ride, noticing her mood altered towards the end of the conversation. He pulled up to the house, turned off the engine, and got out of the car so he could open her door. He held out his hand, waiting for her to get out of the car. After a slight pause, she grabbed his hand and stepped slowly out of the car.

"I think your taxi services are over for the evening. You've done more than enough." Kamryn smiled. She didn't want to get used to this type of treatment, even if only for a night.

"This isn't a taxi service, ma'am. Just the way a man escorts a woman to her home. I need to make sure you've made it safely inside. Your best friend threatened to kill me, remember?"

"Oh, God. You called me 'ma'am.' Do I look as old as I feel?" Kamryn quietly whispered to herself.

"I think you look phenomenal." Ryan responded too quickly.

Kamryn gasped at his comment, not realizing he heard her. She wasn't used to all of this sexual tension between her and Ryan. Or maybe it was just her. Either way, she needed to escape his presence.

"Thank you for driving me home."

Ryan placed his hand on the small of her back again to walk her to the door, and Kamryn felt a chill run through her body. She had to practice some self-control around this man. When they reached the front door, Ryan kept his distance. She couldn't tell if she was disappointed or grateful.

"Duties of a gentleman." Ryan smiled.

Lord, have mercy. Ryan's smile made her insides melt. She felt her body get warm and quickly tried to think of a distraction.

"How long is your drive home?" Kamryn asked.

"About ten minutes. We passed my exit on the way here."

"Oh, I didn't realize. Sorry about that. You should have let me take a cab home so you wouldn't have to pass your house."

"It's no problem. I enjoyed the company."

Kamryn smiled and put her key in the door. "Well, thanks again. Get home safely."

"Thank you. Goodnight."

"Goodnight."

Ryan walked back to his car and started the engine. Kamryn's perfume still lingered in the car even after she left. This was going to be a long ride home.

CHAPTER 8
Home Alone

Jeff sat on the couch, flipping back and forth between CBS and ESPN. Lately, he couldn't find anything on TV, so he usually just sat there and scrolled through all of the channels. This was a rare activity for him since he would normally still be at the office. As he was flipping back and forth, he landed on HGTV and saw a couple knocking down walls with a design team to remodel an old house. This had been one of Kamryn's favorite shows to watch. His memory shifted back to her always hounding him to watch it with her so they could get decorating ideas. It was either HGTV or one of those cooking shows where Kamryn got most of her recipes from. She was always trying to cook something new and get him to try it: vegan casserole, spinach lasagna, lamb burgers, "rainbow" flavored ice cream cupcakes. He had missed a lot of those dinners over the years due to his schedule.

He took a sip of his beer and contemplated calling Kamryn again. It had been over a week since she left him without a single goodbye or notice. She just packed up her stuff and left. He came home from work that day with flowers and two tickets for a vacation to Bora Bora. Kamryn always wanted to go there, but he didn't have the time. He figured this would be a good way to get back into her good graces since she wasn't accepting any of his advances or apologies. When he got home, her car wasn't parked in front, so he figured she was avoiding him and staying at work late. He pulled out his phone to call her as he grabbed a beer from the fridge. That's when he saw the note. He blinked a few times in disbelief and almost spit out his beer. He immediately tried calling her to ask what the meaning of all of this was but didn't get an answer. He raced upstairs and saw something shiny on the bare nightstand. Kamryn's engagement ring.

He looked around the room and suddenly noticed it was empty as well as the dresser, the nightstand, and the broken glass on the floor. The dresser was empty except for his deodorant and cologne. He checked the closets—empty. All of Kamryn's clothes and shoes were gone, including her luggage. She left. He called her job and was told that she had resigned and was on vacation. He suddenly felt like he was living in a twilight zone. He called her cell and texted her but got no reply. He finally called her mother's house after a few days and regretted it instantly. Mrs. Hanover always hated him. After the first time he got caught cheating, Kamryn ran her mouth to her mother, and since then, he'd been her public enemy.

He decided it was time to see Kamryn face-to-face to get to the bottom of this and convince her to come back home. He drove to Kamryn's mother's house, prepared to give her the flowers he purchased a few days ago, but he never got the chance. He had to refrain from grabbing her and throwing her into the car when she refused to listen. He'd been trying to handle this pregnancy situation once he found out. It was his stupid mistake, leaving his phone in the bedroom when Kamryn wasn't home. Jeff was usually quick on his feet, but when he saw her holding his phone and reading the messages, he couldn't do anything but panic. Frozen, he sat there and let the scene play out in his mind again.

******

"Who's Emi?" That's all she said, even though fury was written all over her face.

Jeff remained silent long enough to think of his next move, but nothing came to mind.

"You son of a bitch! You got someone pregnant? AGAIN?!"

He couldn't do anything but stare at her in shock. Her face was covered in tears, and she looked full of rage. When it took him more than ten seconds to respond to her question, Kamryn threw the phone at his chest. Jeff caught it, startled by how hard it hit him, and looked at the open text screen. *Fuck.* He must have mouthed the word because Kamryn started screaming.

"FUCK?! That's all you have to say?! You fucking asshole! How could you do this to me, Jeff? Who the hell is she?!"

Between her crying and screaming, he didn't know what to do first—start explaining, comfort her, or run. He'd never seen her so angry. He decided to go with the comforting tactic since he was not prepared to answer her questions just yet. He took two steps toward her, and she backed away.

"Kamryn, please!"

"Please what, Jeff?! Don't you dare come near me or ask me to calm down! You're so disgusting! It's not enough for you to cheat on me, but you have to keep getting women pregnant, too?!"

"Kamryn, I'm sorry. I didn't mean for this to happen. Just give me a minute to—"

"To what?! Explain?! NO! I don't want to hear you explain. I already saw it. You fucked her, and she got pregnant. Point blank!"

"It was a mistake."

"The only mistake here, Jeff, is you! You're the mistake! This whole entire relationship is a mistake! I can't believe I stayed with you thinking you were going to change. You will never change!"

"Baby, I'm sorry."

"Screw you, screw her, and screw your sorry. Just stay the hell away from me!"

******

Kamryn stormed out of the bedroom and straight through the front door. When he heard the front door slam shut, he figured it was best to not go after her. He thought she would let him explain in the morning, but she didn't. Today was the first time she'd spoken to him in weeks. If only he could make this baby go away; then, he could focus his energy on getting Kamryn back. She was his from the moment he saw her in college, and he wasn't going to just let her go now.

Back in college, she had a few friends that she hung out with, but she mainly stayed in the library or the computer lab, working on projects. She was a member of every club on campus, so in between classes, she was usually busy. Even back then, he knew she would be the perfect wife to settle down with. When he finally convinced her to go on a date with him, he knew he had to do everything in his power to win her over. He smiled thinking about how happy they were back then. Yeah, there were a few women over the years, but he still came home to Kamryn. He provided for her, bought her nice gifts, and proposed to her. He didn't understand why she wouldn't just talk to him. He had invested too much time into Kamryn, and he didn't want to be with anyone else. Emi would just have to understand that they couldn't be together, not like this. Things had become too complicated with the pregnancy. He had been pleading with her for weeks to get rid of the baby for both of their sakes, but she was insisting on keeping it. He offered to pay for everything and arrange for her to go somewhere private to avoid being seen entering a clinic in the city. Of course, he wouldn't be able to go with her because that would put them both at risk.

Outside, Jeff heard a car pull into his driveway and the engine shut off. The driver's door closed, and heeled footsteps approached along the front walkway. Kamryn. Thank God. She had come to her senses and decided to come home. Jeff jumped off the couch and rushed to the front door. He caught his reflection in the hallway mirror and realized he had forgotten to shave this week. He swung open the front door, hoping to greet Kamryn, but was disappointed when he saw who it was.

"What the hell are you doing here?" Jeff asked irritably and out of natural curiosity.

"I came to talk to you. Were you expecting someone else?"

"Just get in." Jeff pulled her in quickly, checking outside for any peeping neighbors.

"So, I'm not allowed to come by anymore?"

"I think you already know the answer to that," Jeff said, unamused by the question.

"You were expecting *her*, weren't you?"

"Does it matter? What are you doing here?" Jeff snapped.

"I know she left you. You forgot that we're friends?"

"Friends?" Jeff scoffs. "Don't forget how our little 'friendship' started. Now, what do you want?"

"Look, I came to talk to you." She paused. "And to tell you that I'm keeping the baby, so you can stop sending me links for abortion clinics." Jeff could tell there was a hint of sarcasm in her voice.

"Are you fucking insane?" He felt his temper flaring.

"Are *you*? You can't just brush this under a rug like you do with all the others. I'm not going to compromise the life of my baby just because you lost your precious girlfriend!"

"And what about you?! Or were you too busy screwing me that you forgot we both have something to lose here. How do you think people will react to this?!"

Jeff's tone was threatening, and he could tell she was holding back tears.

"I thought we had a future. You said that . . ."

"You know we can't be together."

"Only because you care so much about what other people think!"

"And you don't? This could destroy everything!"

"I don't care about—"

"Stop!" Jeff interrupted. "What am I supposed to do? Leave her and flaunt you on my arm? It doesn't work like that!"

Another long pause, she looked down at her hands and started fumbling with her car keys. "I've decided to tell her about the baby. I'm going to tell all of them."

"Get rid of it!" He shouted and took three steps toward where she was standing in the foyer.

"No!" She started to cry, which only made Jeff more frustrated. He had had enough of a woman's tears to last him a lifetime. "This isn't up to you! I'm going to tell her the truth. She deserves to know."

"You can't do that. You'll ruin both of us." Jeff nearly gritted the words through his teeth. He was so close to her face now that she had to step back to avoid them from touching.

"Then, I guess you need to rethink your plans, huh?" She turned on her heels and was out the door before he could speak.

Jeff slammed the door shut, causing the pictures on the walls to rattle. She was trying to force his hand with this pregnancy, and now, his life was falling apart, so he had to get control over this fast. He went to the basement to let off some steam. Martial arts were always a great stress reliever for him ever since high school. His mother had suggested it as a form of therapy since he kept getting into fights. It helped at first. Instead of fighting his classmates, he would take all his energy out in the dojo. He looked forward to his training until he accidentally broke a kid's arm during a match and was kicked out of class. The teacher told his mother that he had exhibited signs of aggression that weren't being resolved through training. So, instead of addressing the issue head-on, his mother enrolled him in another training school across town. After the fifth training school kicked him out, his father told his mother to stop wasting her time and send him to the military. Leave it to his father to suggest sending his son further away.

Robert Rose traveled a lot for business, so he was rarely home to attend to his family's needs, anyway. Julia Rose was too busy pretending things were okay to notice what was going on right under her nose. She ignored the signs—or maybe she saw them and preferred not to address them. Jeff knew he didn't want to leave his home, so he decided to act right long enough to convince his mother that he was capable of change. By the time he was in college, Jeff had mastered the art of manipulation and his ability to convince others. His whole family thought he was on the right track with good grades, the dean's list, and no fights. There was an occasional bar fight or dorm room rumble, but his parents never knew about those. I guess that was the beauty of college: He was able to keep his personal business private. That was until his sister transferred there sophomore year. Lauren was a reminder of the home he was desperately trying to escape.

Jeff tightened his gloves and started to unleash punches on his Century B.O.B. opponent. After a few minutes, the adrenaline was pumping, and he felt his muscles getting looser. He was starting to feel better already. Fighting had always done that for him; similarly, sex had been a release for him, too. Admittedly, he'd been careless over the years, but sex had always been his biggest escape.

He thought he could develop some sense of normalcy with Kamryn, but when his stress levels went up, he always needed more. He didn't need to see a therapist to know that he was a sex addict, although he had seen a therapist who confirmed it. A "sex addict with major destructive and depressive behaviors" is what Dr. Nolan said exactly. Jeff continued to punch with intensity. He made a few threats over the years, but that was only to prevent women from trying to trap him. He didn't want to have a baby with anyone but Kamryn. He loved her, and, ultimately, she would be his wife. With Kamryn, he could have the real thing—a real family.

So, if he had to threaten a few lives to get his way, he would do just that. Eventually, they all came around. A few nights in a cage could change anyone's mind. He started to punch and kick harder, now feeling the burn in his legs. His phone started to ring in his pocket. He let out two more punches before checking the caller ID: Julia Rose. Crap. Just what I need, he thought. He decided not to answer and kept punching. Besides, he didn't have much to say to his mother. Their relationship had become almost as strained as the relationship with his father. He knew why she was calling, and he didn't have time for that conversation yet. He had to deal with his first problem at hand.

He took a break and walked over to his wall cabinet. He normally kept it locked, but since Kamryn moved out, he didn't have a reason to anymore. He sifted through the pill bottles until he found what he was looking for, Mifepristone. He'd stolen a script pad from Dr. Nolan to stock up his medicine cabinet. Guess the good doctor was useful after all. It had been a while since he needed to resort to this, but he couldn't risk losing everything, his career, reputation, and Kamryn. They just needed a fresh start. He held the pill bottles in hand while his phone continued ringing in his pocket. He pressed the "Ignore" button and stuffed the bottles into his pocket.

When his phone chimed again, Jeff considered answering just to end the calls from his mother. Instead, he saw two Instagram alerts from @SweetMica and @NickiBabez. Jeff made it a point to follow all of Kamryn's friends when they started dating. He found out more about them through their social media pages than Kamryn would ever tell him. He set up post alerts to keep tabs on Kamryn when she hung out with her friends, since she didn't post a lot. Jeff didn't care for Michelle and Nicole, and he was sure the feeling was mutual and that they were probably the ones convincing her to leave him.

He opened Michelle's post first: a selfie and a group photo of her, Nicole, Kamryn, Charles and two other guys. He vaguely remembered the guy's faces from some parties he went to with Kamryn over the years. He studied the picture and noticed that he hadn't seen Kamryn ever wear that dress. In fact, he hadn't seen Kamryn dress like that at all. Obviously Michelle's and Nicole's influence, he thought. He checked Nicole's post next, and he saw the same group photo, plus another group picture where Kamryn was standing closer to one of the guys. They looked comfortable. His hands were around her waist, she was smiling, and her chest was pressed against him. Jeff clutched his phone so tightly he thought it would break in his hand. Is she already seeing someone else? Has she been seeing this guy the whole time?

He went back to the medicine cabinet and grabbed the Trazodone, something Dr. Nolan had prescribed. He popped two pills and stared at the picture on his phone. Guess he was back to his old ways after all.

CHAPTER 9
All work, No play

M onday morning came and went. In fact, the whole week at Alpine Bloom had been a blur. Thank goodness it was Friday. I spent the entire week in training, shadowing, and updating my portfolio with new design sketches for our current project. My boss, Margaret Stone, the VP of Marketing, was the definition of a workhorse. She was relentless in her search for new clientele to take Alpine Bloom to the next level. She was finally able to seal a deal to represent a hotel chain in the area, Ambi Luxe Hotels. They had a few locations along the east coast, mostly in the northeast region, and Alpine Bloom was now the head of their marketing redesign for all their locations. Margaret had been on top of the team for the last week with reminders to submit our design proposals by the deadline, which was today. I was pleased with what I came up with but also apprehensive about my designs since this was my first-time submitting ideas for consideration. Margaret put together an executive design team, all of whom came with extensive portfolios and experience. All I had was a few degrees and a previous position at a law firm that held no significance to my experience other than the misleading title of "Senior Marketing Specialist."

After I submitted my portfolio, the rest of the day was pretty much a bore. I found myself occasionally thinking of Ryan. I thought of him a lot, actually: the way his hand touched my back, the way I kept catching him looking at me, and the way he kept slightly readjusting his pants or shirt when he was uncomfortable. I inhaled at my desk, thinking about the scent of his cologne and the strength in his arms when he hugged me. Interestingly, I had never seen him in a sexual light. Not that he wasn't attractive; he just had a repulsive personality at times. He appeared to be a stereotypical guy who leads with his smaller head first, which makes sense, considering some of the women he's dated and how he was sexualizing me last weekend. From what I could tell, he kept a healthy rotation of women on his arm, which left me curious as to why he would be suddenly flirting with me. As I considered his reputation more, I realized that he may be as promiscuous as Jeff. No, he wasn't my type at all; he was arrogant, distasteful, and, not to mention, insufferable every time I spoke to him.

Just then, my phone vibrated my entire desk, scaring me nearly half to death and out of my romantic daydream. I didn't realize how long I had been thinking about Ryan until I looked at my phone—nearly fifteen minutes. I checked my phone to see a message in the group chat again.

Mica: Hey, Kam! You've been M.I.A. all week . . . What's up? *Angry face emojis*

Kamryn: Sorry! I've been up early and sleeping late trying to finish these proposals. *Sleepy emoji*

Nicole: Mm-hmm . . . Have you been sleeping alone lately? *Smirk emoji*

Leave it to Nicole to sexualize everything, I thought.

Kamryn: Of course, I have . . . Who else am I going to sleep with In my mom's house??

Nicole: RYAN!

Mica: LOL . . . yes, RYAN!

Nicole: Mm-hmm . . . I saw the way he was checking you out at NOVA. I

bet he couldn't wait to get you home. *Smirk emoji*

Kamryn: What? *Eye roll emoji* He wasn't checking me out. We barely even spoke . . .

Nicole: Not a lot of talking usually means there is a lot of something else going on.

LOL . . . *wink emoji*

Kamryn: *eye roll emoji* That was a week ago, ladies. Give it up already!

Lauren: OMG . . . What did I miss?

Kamryn: Absolutely nothing, Lauren.

Mica: Ks got a new crush . . . LOL. *Kissy face emoji*

Kamryn: No, thanks. Not interested. Next subject, please.

Lauren: What? Who's the new beau?

Mica: Scroll up, Lauren.

Nicole: Sure, K, whatever you say. Any who, a couple apartments opened in a new complex up in Windsor Heights and Essex Commons. They're doing renovations, but it should be ready in a few weeks if you're interested.

Kamryn: Seriously?! YES! When can I see it?

Nicole: Once the renovations are done, I'll take you.

Kamryn: Thanks, Nic! *Red heart emoji*

Nicole: *kissy face emoji*

Mica: Are you ladies still coming over tonight for drinks? I have a case of reds and whites left over from my teacher's retreat, and I don't want to drink it alone.

Nicole: Count me in . . .

Kamryn: Yeah, I'll be there.

Lauren: Okay! *Thumbs up emoji*

It was great having friends who cared enough to help you out. Nicole Stewart was one of the top real estate agents in the county. After college, she started working for an insurance company and mastered the trade of home and auto insurance. After a while, she got bored and decided to take classes and get her real estate license. Being the risk taker that she was, Nicole loved the fluctuating risks of real estate. She flourished in it. Once she heard that I was leaving Jeff and would need a place of my own very soon, she was on the hunt.

Natalie: Omg . . . I missed a lot at NOVA. Kamryn's hot for Ryan? LOL! Go, girl! See y'all tonight!

Natalie Graham was always the late comer to a text because she was either birthing babies or burping babies. Nat didn't waste any time after college, settling down and starting a family. She and hubby were already expecting baby number three. I didn't even bother to respond because that would have welcomed another onslaught of texts about Ryan. It was best to leave it alone and squash all lingering rumors later tonight.

Luckily, I didn't have to see him that often or even at all. We didn't run in the same social circles outside of knowing Mica and Charlie, and that circle of friends didn't get together that often—or maybe they did, and I just wasn't around. There were a couple of functions that I missed due to me being in a relationship. Actually, there were more than a couple. Jeff always complained about hanging out with my friends or being around people outside of his typical circle. Most of our outings were with his company buddies and corporate functions. When we went out with my friends, he would find himself a bar and drink to avoid having to socialize. However, the drinks only made him obnoxious, so to avoid embarrassment, I stayed in and turned down the invites. I tried to attend most of the girls' nights, which Jeff loved because I would usually stay over at Mica's or Nicole's, so he was free to roam the streets and do as he please.

I checked the clock on my computer and it was already 4:50 p.m. I must have lost track of time somewhere between searching the internet for apartments and daydreaming of Ryan.

"Hey, Kamryn. Got any plans tonight?" Daniel slumped his body over the partition by my desk. He was one of the marketing associates in my department. He was nice enough, always offering to get me coffee, pick up lunch, or walk me to my car when we stayed late.

"Not really. Just getting together with a few of my girlfriends."

"That's cool. You get to talk about all the men in your lives and bash them, right?"

"Pretty much. What about you? Any plans this weekend?"

"Not really. I was thinking about going to see that new Anthony Hopkins movie that just came out. Have you seen it?"

"No. I don't get out that much."

"Oh, we'll have to change that. You want to see it this weekend?"

Is he asking me out on a date? Dating people, I work with is an obvious no-no, especially as a newbie. The best way to start a rumor is to be seen spending too much time with or being overly friendly to a coworker. And I knew from experience with Jeff's gossiping colleagues that everyone sees everything.

"No, thanks. I have some apartment hunting to do."

"Okay, cool. Maybe another time. Get home safe."

And with that, he walked off toward the elevator, pausing to give a quick wave to Margaret and Abigail, our freelance photographer. I tossed my phone in my purse and finished packing up so I could head home for a quick shower and to pack a bag. I would most likely be staying over at Mica's house tonight after drinking wine and dishing secrets all night.

"Hi, Margaret. I'm heading out for the day. Do you need any help with anything?"

"No, thanks. It's been a busy week. Enjoy your weekend."

"Thank you. Same to you." I turned to keep walking to the elevator until she called me back.

"Kamryn, I glanced over your portfolio you submitted today. Pretty impressive. Good work."

"Oh, wow. Thank you so much. Have a good night."

"Goodnight," Margaret and Abbi both say in unison.

✶✶✶✶✶✶

As soon as I pulled up to Mica's house, my Spidey-senses immediately went off—not just because I saw Ryan's car, but because my entire body started tingling at the thought of being so close to him again. What the hell is he doing here? And why didn't Mica tell me? I rang the doorbell, feeling slightly annoyed and excited about his presence.

Charlie answered the door. "Hey! Look who made it! Come in, come in. Let me take your bag."

"Hey, Charlie. How are you?"

"Not in a pool of water, so I guess I'm doing great."

Good old Charlie. Always pleasant, even if it didn't make sense. I walked into the living room and found everyone sitting around, laughing and screaming rather than talking. Mica noticed me and jumped up from her seat.

"Kam Kam! I was wondering when you were going to get here. Come, let's get you a drink." Kam was a name my parents called me when they were about to give me bad news: once when my grandmother passed away, and then again when they were telling me about their divorce. Mica knew that, and I guess she was prepared to explain how this girls' night turned into an "all of us" party.

After waving hello to everyone and being whisked away into the kitchen, I pulled my arm away from Michelle's grasp.

"What the hell, Mica? Why the hell is he here?"

"I'm sorry. Charlie's place flooded this afternoon, and they haven't finished cleaning everything up yet. So, the guys came over here to take a break and get a drink."

"And you couldn't give me a heads-up?"

"Would you have come if I told you he was here?" Mica asked and gave me a look that told me she already knew the answer.

"No, but you still should have told me. Besides, why can't they go to one of their own houses?"

"Because we already have beer and food. Plus, I thought it would be nice if we had a little game night."

"Well, I don't think this is fun at all."

"Have a drink, Kam. It'll be fun before you know it."

"Don't call me that. You know I hate it."

Mica chuckled, obviously getting a kick out of my discomfort. "It'll be fun. I promise. "

I reluctantly dragged my feet back into the living room and found a seat on the opposite side of Ryan, who was staring a hole through me. His incessant gaze was so obvious now that I was positive everyone could tell. It felt as if there was a spotlight on the both of us every time, we locked eyes. I took a sip of my wine to break the trance and attempted to focus on the game going on in the rest of the room.

"You know y'all are cheating, right? You can't put a draw four on a draw two!" Drew yelled.

"Yes, you can, if it's the same color! Read the rule book!" Nicole laughed.

"There is no rule book! You ladies are making up the rules as you go and cheating."

"I've never seen an Uno rule book. Maybe that's why we're always losing," Charlie chimed in.

"You guys didn't set the rules before you started the game?" I asked.

"Yes. He's just mad that he sucks and keeps losing." Mica laughed.

"Andrew, why do you always pick this game, knowing that you're no good at it?" Natalie asked with a hint of sweet sarcasm.

"I am good at it. I only lose when I'm here with you ladies. That's how I know you're all cheating," Drew responded.

"Well, pick up your six cards or place another yellow card down so we can move on," Nicole chuckled.

"I quit." Drew tossed his hand of cards onto the table and stood up.

"Ahhh, don't be a sore loser!" Mica yelled while everyone else laughed.

"I'm not; I just have to take a whiz. I'll be back refreshed."

"I'll take his turn. Deal me in." I kneeled to get a comfortable space on the floor cushions closer to Mica's coffee table.

"That means you'll have to draw six cards," Ryan chimed in.

I looked up to meet his gaze again, and I felt Nicole snickering behind her cards next to me.

"That's no problem. I'm not scared," I said as lightheartedly as I could.

"That's right, Ryan. Keep her in check." Nicole smiled as she handed me the extra cards.

I resisted the urge to roll my eyes at her or make eye contact with Ryan again.

"Just deal the cards so I can show you how it's done."

CHAPTER 10
Game Night

Three hours later, I could barely stand. Between the wine, margaritas, and occasional shots, I was over my normal limit. I was slouched on the chair, laughing at one of Drew's jokes when I thought I almost peed my pants.

"OMG! Drew, you are so gross! Where do you meet these women?" Natalie yelled out.

"What? It's not my fault she couldn't hold it," Drew said in self-defense.

"The way you guys sit here and talk about women makes me happy to have male friends. I always know what not to do on a date," Nicole chimed in.

"We don't talk any worse than you ladies. Heck, we learned it from y'all," Andrew barked back.

"Exactly right! You ladies love to dog us," Charlie said as Mica shot him a look.

"Oh, please. Who's dogging you, Charlie? You're a part of the premier gentlemen's club. You wouldn't hurt a fly, and the ladies know it," Drew added.

"That's right, and I'm a lucky man because of it." Charlie and Mica shared a kiss that made the rest of us gag and look away.

"Get a room already," Lauren stated as she rolled her eyes in disgust.

"Even if they don't dog us, they jump to conclusions about us and make us pay for their assumptions later," Ryan said. He looked at me while sipping his beer as if he was baiting me to respond.

"You got a point there, man," Drew agreed.

I took the bait. "What assumptions do women make about you, Ryan?" I asked while sipping my drink.

He smirked. "You know, they assume I'm shallow because I dated one Victoria's Secret model."

"And you're not?"

"Not what?"

"Shallow?"

"No, but you should get to know me and find out for yourself."

In a room full of people, I couldn't take my eyes off Ryan. This was becoming too intense. Did he just say that in front of all these people? What is he insinuating?

"Shallow? Ryan? Definitely not. He's deep—real deep. And the ladies love him for it. Right, Ryan?" Drew gave Ryan a sly smirk and patted him on the shoulder as if to congratulate him for being a playboy.

"I don't know about all of that," Ryan responded, visibly embarrassed.

"Don't be modest, Ryan. We all know you're a playa, playa," I added.

"I get it. It's a lot to deal with. He *is* your brother."

"I know Jeff can be a handful. I wish I could have done more to protect you from this."

"It's not on you, Lauren. In fact, it has nothing to do with you. I'm sorry if you feel like you're caught in the crosshairs."

Lauren takes a long pause and looked down at her feet. When she looked back up at me, I saw that she was worried about something.

"Are you okay? If you're worried about me going back to Jeff, trust me—that's not going to happen."

"Just stay away from him. There's a lot you don't know about him. He can be . . . dangerous."

"I don't plan on going back to him or being anywhere near him. Are you sure you're okay?"

She opened her mouth as if to say something, then changed her mind.

"Yeah. Just tired, I guess. It's been a long week, so I'm going to head home soon." She moved past me and went into the restroom. Strange. I had never seen Lauren so concerned about me and Jeff. Did he say something to her to make her uncomfortable?

I walked back into the living room and saw Natalie trying to get up from the couch with her pregnant belly.

"Leaving us, Nat?" I asked.

"Yeah, girl. I have to get home to my babies. James already texted me three times."

"Aww. He misses you."

"No, he just has no clue what to do with kids while I'm gone."

"Call us when you get home!" Mica yelled as she continued to kiss Charlie.

"Sure will. It's been fun watching y'all drink and make fools of yourselves." Natalie laughed at her own joke and waddled towards the bathroom.

"I think I'm going to head out, too. That last shot has me feeling a little sick." Nicole held her stomach.

"I'm right behind you, Nic. Let me just try to straighten up a little." I started picking up glasses to take into the kitchen.

"Wait, what? You're not staying over?" Wow. Mica broke away from Charlie long enough to ask us a question.

"No! You clearly need the place to yourself tonight, girl." Nic did her little humping dance and blew a kissy face at Mica and Charlie.

"We've all been drinking, so no. You two are definitely spending the night!" Mica exclaimed.

"Don't sweat it, Mica. I'll Uber home and come back and get my car in the morning. Enjoy your man." I winked at her to give her some extra reassurance. If nothing else, Michelle Canmore was loyal to the core, and nothing came before her girls.

"I'm heading home, too. Anyone need a ride?" Lauren emerged from the bathroom hallway.

"ME!" Nic threw her hand up like we were in a classroom.

"Wait, were you drinking rosé?" Mica questioned. Calling us by our last name usually meant she means business.

"Nope. I'm sober. Still recovering from that stomach bug."

"Cool. Let's roll." Nicole stumbled towards the door.

"Please don't throw up in my car, Nicole. I just had it cleaned," Lauren pleaded.

"Drew, wake up. Let's roll!" Ryan shouted for Andrew, who was snoring on the couch.

"When did he fall asleep?" I asked. I was surprised, considering he was yelling a few moments ago.

"Who knows? He can't hold his liquor for shit." Ryan picked up the remaining glasses and followed me into the kitchen.

"Apparently, you can. You seem completely sober."

"I try not to get drunk in the presence of a goddess. The devil in me might come out."

He was standing so close to me when he spoke that I could feel his breath on my ear. If I turned around now, our lips might touch. I continued to rinse the glass and load the dishwasher.

"Wait, I saw you drink, like, seven beers and throw back a few shots with no chaser. How are you sober?"

"I'll tell you my secret in the car."

"I'm calling an Uber, so there's no need—"

"Are we really going to do this again?" he asked while cutting me off mid-sentence. "You tell me you're calling an Uber while I keep insisting to drive you home."

I turned to look at him this time. He was serious. Painstakingly gorgeous, but very serious. How did anyone resist a face like this? How will I?

"Has anyone ever told you that you're bossy?" I asked.

"Caring, maybe. But not bossy."

"Is that what you call it?"

"Yup. So, are you going to keep fighting me?"

"I guess not," I answered him.

"Good. Let me go get this lush in the car, and I'll meet you outside."

I heard Ryan say his goodbyes and called Andrew to wake him up again. Andrew must have knocked something over in his attempt to stand up because I heard things shatter on the floor as Mica walked in the kitchen to check on me.

"Are you sure you're not staying? You know Charlie's ass can go home."

"No. Stop it. Why should you sleep alone because this spinster doesn't have a man?"

Mica shot me a disapproving look.

"It's fine. Ryan is going to give me a ride."

"Hmm . . . That's two weekends in a row, huh?" Mica raised her eyebrows and started poking me in the arm.

I rolled my eyes so hard that my head started to hurt. "Would you stop it already?"

"I'm just saying. Maybe I won't be the only one snuggled up tonight after all," Mica laughed.

"Bye, Michelle." I walked out the kitchen, grabbed my things, and headed for the door, with Mica right on my heels.

Ryan was waiting by the passenger side door. What is with this guy? Who is he trying to impress? Over my shoulder, I heard Mica yelling.

"Goodnight, you two! Ryan, make sure my friend gets home safely. Kamryn, feel free to text me in the morning if you're too *tired* tonight!"

I kept walking, pretending not to hear her, although I'm sure the whole neighborhood heard her. Ryan opened the door, and I slid in the passenger seat. Immediately, I was greeted by Andrew's snoring in the back seat.

Ryan

"He's out cold, huh?" she asked.

"Yeah. He's either running his mouth or sleeping when he's drunk. There's no in between."

"So, are you going to tell me your secret now, since you're clearly sober?" Kamryn looked over at him and folded her arms. God, she's beautiful, even when drunk, he thought.

"I fill my beer bottle up with water all night."

"What?! You're kidding!" Kamryn's eyes were squinted low, and she let out a hearty laugh that Ryan rarely heard.

"Nope; I'm serious. I usually drink the first one, and then I refill it with water in the kitchen all night. The trick is to get your own drink every time you're running low so no one else can bring you one."

"OMG! That's so crazy!" she said with her eyes still half-open. Kamryn reclined her chair back a little. "And what about the shots? I saw you do at least three!"

"I throw them behind me."

That sent her over the top. She laughed so hard that tears started to form in her eyes. Ryan checked the back seat through the rearview mirror to see if Andrew woke up. Luckily, he was still in hibernation.

"You WHAT?! OMG! That's so clever." Kamryn was getting louder. Ryan turned to look at the cute, loud drunk in his passenger seat. Still a goddess, he thought.

"Yeah, it usually works unless someone is behind me. I messed that up a few times in college," Ryan confessed. He usually didn't share this much, but he could tell that Kamryn was intrigued, and at least he had made her laugh.

"It's so hot." Kamryn tugged on her shirt and lifted it up slightly to reveal her belly button. Ryan turned on the AC and shifted his thoughts back to the road. He had been tempted to touch her all night. All night, he sat and watched her drink, laugh, and do impromptu dance moves with Nicole, Lauren, and Michelle. She was so lively. He wondered how he hadn't noticed this before.

"Is the air okay?"

"It's a little cold." Kamryn's eyes were completely closed now, and she was rubbing her hands over her arms. Ryan turned off the AC and cracked the window.

"Is that better?" Ryan looked over at Kamryn again to catch her nodding off slightly. God, she's even cute while she's sleeping. She was going to drive him insane.

As he kept staring at her, he began wondering again what it would be like to kiss her, hold her hand, and caress her fingers. He wanted to touch her so badly. He felt himself becoming aroused just by looking at her. Then, she moaned out loud and turned on her side, facing him, still fast asleep. He kept having the urge to pull over and make love to her in the car or, better yet, bring her back home with him. Andrew shifted in the back seat and let out a snort, snapping Ryan back to reality. He checked on his friend through the rearview mirror again. Even in his sleep, Andrew was still a cock blocker.

It was probably for the best, anyway. He learned through different conversations tonight that she had just broken up with Jeff, and he was pretty certain that those wounds were still fresh. She was also Charlie's girlfriend's best friend. That was too close for comfort. Ryan preferred to keep his friendships and sex life private. If he started sleeping with Kamryn, the whole crew would know. But damn, he wanted her more now than ever. *What is it about this woman that I can't shake?* He turned to look at her again and was startled to see her bright brown eyes looking back at him, seemingly fully awake.

"Hey . . . You're awake?" he asked.

"Sorry. I didn't realize I fell asleep." She turned back to face forward and pulled the seat back to its original position, looking slightly uncomfortable.

"Did you have a good dream?"

"What?" Kamryn asked, taken aback.

"You seemed like you were dreaming when you were asleep. A good one, I hope."

"Uh, yeah. I guess so. Was I talking?" Ryan could tell she was embarrassed, so he decided to play with her a little.

"A little this, a little that. A few moans here and there."

"Oh, my God." Kamryn placed her hand on her head and closed her eyes again.

"Care to share?" Ryan asked with a smirk to help lighten the mood.

"No, definitely not. Are we close?"

Not what he was expecting. "Yeah. Just a few minutes."

She was clearly having an erotic dream. He could tell by the way her body curled up in the seat and the sinister grin on her face while she slept. The moan was also a dead giveaway. Was it a dream about him? Or maybe her ex? Of course. She was dreaming about her ex, and why wouldn't she be? She had been with him for years and could barely stand to be around Ryan for more than a few minutes. He thought he felt a spark between them last week but was evidently mistaken. She wasn't into him, and she made that painfully clear in more ways than one, especially if she was still dreaming of her ex.

He pulled over in front of her house, and before he could put the car in park, Kamryn opened the door.

"Hey. Hold on a sec." By the time he made it around the car, she was halfway to her front door.

"Kamryn."

She stopped and turned around. "Sorry. I'm just a little tired. Thanks for the ride home." She was clearly trying to avoid him now.

"Are you okay?"

"Sure."

"I didn't mean to make you uncomfortable about your dream. I was only joking around."

"Oh. It's fine." She turned back around and pulled her keys out of her purse.

"So, what time tomorrow?" he asked.

"What time for what?"

"To take you back to Michelle's house. You have to go pick up your car, right?"

Kamryn paused and stared at him for a few seconds. "You're kidding, right?"

"No," Ryan responded with a straight face, daring her to test him again tonight.

"I'll let you know," Kamryn responded.

Ryan felt his heart tingle. He watched Kamryn walk away for the third time, trying to escape. As she put her key in the door, he stopped her one last time.

"Kamryn." She turned around. "Sweet dreams," he said with a grin that sent her running in the house.

CHAPTER 11
Dinner & Deception

The next morning, I woke up with my head still spinning and a constant ringing in my ears. I rolled over and pulled the cover over my head. Glancing at the alarm clock, I saw it was 12:48 p.m. Why the heck is my alarm going off on a Saturday? I hit the snooze with more force than normal, and the whole clock fell to the floor. I sat up slightly and realized my cell phone was making all of the noise. I grabbed my phone and squinted at the caller ID. Whoever this is was going to pay. Mica.

"Hello?" I answer, sounding obviously irritated.

"I know you're not still asleep at one in the afternoon. Ryan must have given you one hell of a ride home." Mica laughed into the phone.

"Shut it. Now, how can I help you?"

"We're supposed to be going shopping, or did you forget?"

"Ugh. No, I remember. I just overslept. Remind me to never drink one of your margaritas again. I swear you're adding more than tequila."

"Of course I am. That's why they're so good." We both laugh into the phone.

"What time do you want to head out?"

"As soon as you get your butt over here. You left your car here, remember? And I can't drive it to you because you took the keys."

"Oh, yeah. Right." Another one of my bright ideas. "Let me shower and get my life together. I'll call you when I'm in the Uber."

"All right. See you soon."

I hung up and lay back down to try and snooze for a few minutes until my phone started vibrating and ringing again. A text from Mica.

Mica: GET UP!

Ugh! This girl made me sick with how well she knew me. I angrily snatched off the covers and nearly stomped into the bathroom before I remembered my mother may be home. No need to disturb her with my crankiness.

After a twenty-minute shower, I looked almost human again. I walked over to my closet to grab a dress, and I heard my phone ringing again. Mica was becoming relentless. I snatched my phone off the bed, and to my surprise, it was not Michelle.

"Hello?"

"Hey, Kamryn."

"Hey, Jenny. How are you?" It had been a few weeks since we last spoke.

"I'm doing okay. I just wanted to check in with you and see how you were doing." I noticed that she didn't sound like her regular self.

"Yeah, I know. I haven't had a chance to reach back out to you in a couple of weeks. Just been busy with the move and the new job. Sorry about that."

"No worries. It's really me who should be apologizing to you. I've been trying to give you space. But I'm hoping we can catch up."

Speaking to Jenny reminded me of my past. The last time we spoke, I was canceling our dinner plans because I had just broken up with Jeff. She called to confirm and heard me sniffling through the phone. I ended up telling her everything. She didn't even seem surprised. Maybe because everyone knew that Jeff was a cheater, and I was the last to hear about it this time.

"Sure. It's been a while."

"Are you free today?"

"I'm actually heading to the mall in a few, but we can have dinner later. Around 7:00-ish?

"That works for me," Jenny agreed.

"Okay; sounds good. I'll text you the address, but let me know if you think of a different place."

I didn't think it would be this hard to face people from my past. Jenny was a good friend, but talking to her instantly brought me back to the conversations we used to have about Jeff and David, and I was trying to stay clear of all things Jeff. I guess a quick dinner at the mall couldn't hurt. Plus, I'd have Mica there as a buffer just in case.

******

"I can't believe you made me buy all this mess!"

"What mess? You mean the shoes, perfumes, underwear, and bras that you so desperately needed?" Mica asked.

"I have cute underwear and bras, thank you," I responded.

"Yes, but those have already been infiltrated by the enemy. You need new stuff just in case . . . you know." Mica nudged me in the arm.

"Uh-uh. That's not going to happen. I told you I need to focus."

"So, that means you can't indulge?" Mica questioned.

"YES! Precisely. I'm not interested in him, anyway."

"Who?"

"Ryan," I responded nonchalantly as I skimmed the aisles for dresses.

"Who said anything about Ryan?"

I turned to find Michelle staring at me with a questionable look.

"I just assumed that's who you were talking about . . . Do you like this?" I asked, holding up a black dress.

"Stop lying, Kamryn. Did y'all do it? Oh, my God! I knew it!" Mica was in between a whisper and a scream.

"Nooo, we didn't. I would have told you." I kept holding up the dress, waiting for a yes or a no.

"So, what aren't you telling me?" Mica snatched the dress from my hands and hung it back on the rack.

"Ugh. I had a wet dream about him," I said as we headed out of the store.

"Okay, and? What's the big deal?" Mica seemed unimpressed.

"I had the dream right in front of him while he was driving me home last night. I must have dozed off, and my mind wandered. It was so intense. By the time I got inside the house, I was soaked, literally."

Mica's mouth was hanging open, and on this a rare occasion, nothing was coming out.

"Mica, stop. You're only making me feel worse."

"Girl, that's really embarrassing. Even for me." I could tell she was trying not to laugh—unsuccessfully.

"I know. And to make matters worse, he asked me about it when I woke up."

"No, he did not!"

"Yes, he did. And you know I talk in my sleep when I'm really tired. So, there's no telling what I said."

"Oh, my God, Kamryn! I mean, as embarrassing as that is, at least he knows that you want him now, so, he can make the first move."

"What? Who said that? I don't want him; I just had a little dream. That's all."

"Mm-hmm. I think that dream was trying to communicate something you can't."

"Well, it's never happening again. As long as I stay away from him, I won't have to worry about that."

"Sure. What time are we having dinner with your friend? Jennifer, right?"

"Yeah. I told her around 7:00." I took out my cell phone and checked the time—6:43 p.m. I texted Jenny to see if she was close by. She answered back right away, saying that she was parking her car near the food court entrance. I told her to meet me at the Japanese restaurant, since I had a craving for teriyaki and Mica mentioned wanting sushi earlier.

"She's here. She's going to meet us at the Japanese place."

"Okay, great. I've been dying for some good sushi."

Mica and I got there a few minutes before Jenny and grabbed a booth. When Jenny walked in and approached the table, she looked a little disappointed. The look quickly turned into a smile when she noticed me staring, but I caught it. Everyone exchanged pleasantries, and after a few minutes, we were drinking sake and waiting for our food.

"So, what's new with you? Write any new plays?" I asked in a failed attempt to avoid the obvious conversations.

"No, not yet. I've still been busy with the cast for the last play. You look great, Kamryn. What have you been up to?"

"A little bit of this, a little bit of that. Mostly work, though."

Mica smirked over her drink. I knew she thought I was talking about Ryan.

"How's the new job coming along?" Jenny asked.

"It's okay. It's only been a week, and it's already busy. But it's nice to be back in my field of work."

She looked down at her water glass and hesitated for a moment before speaking again.

"That's good." She glanced at Mica, then back at me. Another awkward pause. "Have you talked to Jeff?"

Now, I was the one with the awkward pause. Mica stopped sipping her sake long enough to give both me and Jenny hard looks.

"No, not recently. We exchanged a few words a week ago, but nothing since then."

"He hasn't tried to reach out to you?"

"He calls, but I don't answer. Has David said anything to you?"

"No," she answered, gazing around the restaurant.

"Figures. They only speak about work. Everything else just falls off their radar. How is David, anyway?"

"He's okay, I guess." She paused before deciding to continue. "I think we're getting a divorce."

"What?! Why? You two were so happy." I was shocked to think that Jenny would divorce David. She had very much been the devoted wife over the years.

"We were happy once, but . . . I want more. And there's just some things that he won't commit to." Her eyes started to swell, and I could tell she was on the brink of tears.

"I'm really sorry to hear that. I could sense something was wrong over the phone. Is that what you wanted to talk about?"

Jenny looked away from the table, as if fighting the urge to cry again. Michelle kicked my leg under the table, and I shot her a glare. I was at a loss for words and didn't know how to comfort Jenny. Yeah, I had just walked away from a relationship, but this was different. David and Jennifer Lancaster were married and were never seen even having a disagreement. I guess some things couldn't work themselves out.

"Yeah. I didn't want to call you about my drama when you were still going through it with Jeff. I guess I just needed to get it out for once."

"How does David feel about this?" Mica asked.

"He doesn't know. I haven't worked up the nerve to tell him yet."

"Are you absolutely sure you want to do this, Jenny? Don't you think you can just talk to him? I'm sure David will try to understand, whatever it is."

"No, he won't. There's no coming back from this."

The waiter came to our table with our orders, and the conversation halted. But those words, "There's no coming back from this," played over in my head. Had David cheated on Jenny, too? Maybe Jeff had influenced his boss after all.

We ate most of our food in silence until Mica mentioned that she wanted to check out the new iPhone that just released. She was thinking about getting Charlie a new phone for his birthday in a few months.

"If I start paying for it now, maybe I'll have it paid off in ten years."

"Yeah, those phones are crazy expensive, all for just a small device," Jenny added.

The conversation remained light and uneventful for about forty-five minutes. The waiter brought the check, and we all reached in our purses to pull out our cash or cards.

"Oh, my God. I love your wallet. Is that the new LV monogram?" Mica asked Jenny.

"Yeah, I got it around the holidays." Jenny suddenly looked uncomfortable.

The wallet was checkered brown with a small gold LV emblem on the front and pink lining on the side. The inside was also pink with the initials "J.E.L." ascribed (or engraved or monogrammed) on the front.

"Even with a sale, that thing is probably about $1,500." Mica said, admiring the wallet.

"I have a purse from there that Jeff bought me a while ago. I told him he could have purchased a zip code for what he paid for it," I added.

Mica and Jenny laughed, which made me feel like Jenny's mood was improving.

"Especially with the extra engraving," Mica said, still admiring the wallet. "Didn't Jeff engrave almost every gift he bought you?" Mica asked.

"Yes. Wallets, bags, belts! He even engraved a shirt once. I guess it was his way of showing attention or affection."

"Yeah, by remembering your name." Mica rolled her eyes and laughed at her own statement. We were both laughing, and I noticed that Jenny's mood had shifted again.

"I'm going to use the restroom. This is my treat, ladies. Can you just give the waiter my card when he comes back?" Before we could protest, Jenny was up from the table and heading towards the restrooms.

"That was awkward," Mica said.

"This whole situation is awkward. I don't know why I agreed to this."

"Look, you can't avoid everyone who knew you when you were with Jeff. Just think of this as one of your steps."

"Steps to what?" I asked.

"Steps to getting over Jeff. The next step is to get under Ryan."

I elbowed Mica in her side as she laughed at her own stupid joke.

After the bill was settled and Jenny returned from the restroom, we walked back into the food court. Mica and I were parked by Nordstrom, so we had to hike back to the other end of the mall.

"Thanks for dinner, Jenny. It was nice to catch up. Hopefully, we can do it again in better circumstances."

"I'm going to miss seeing you at those boring galas, but I guess I won't be attending, either."

I noticed she didn't agree to my suggestion of hanging out again. Mica's phone rang, and she strolled off to take a call, probably from Charlie.

"Are you sure you're, okay? I know this all can't be easy," I asked.

"Yeah. I guess I'm just getting used to the idea of everything. I think I'm going to get away for a while." Jenny looked as if she wanted to cry again.

"Maybe that's what you and David need, a getaway."

"No, I mean relocate and start over—without David. I've contemplated packing my bags and catching a plane somewhere just to escape."

"I know it's rough. It took me a few weeks to come to terms that I was leaving Jeff. Every day felt like it was harder than the last. But eventually, it will get easier. Just make sure this is what you really want," I urged.

"Kamryn, it's not that." Jenny allowed the tears to flow from her eyes. "I wanted to tell you before, but I saw Michelle, and I lost my nerve."

"Tell me what?"

Mica started walking towards us again, looking smitten after her call with Charlie.

"I'm pregnant," Jenny said flatly through her tears.

"Oh, my God! Congratulations! I knew you were trying; this is great!"

Jenny's tears ran more forcibly down her cheeks. Mica started digging in her purse, looking for something to give Jenny to wipe her tears.

"This is good news, right?" I asked, trying to cheer her up while rubbing her shoulders.

"No." Jenny was shaking her head and trying to wipe her tears.

"Why?" I asked, confused.

"It's Jeff's."

CHAPTER 12
Who's Emi?

I felt like someone punched me in the stomach, and as I doubled over in pain, someone else kicked me in the face. Shock, confusion, hurt, and, most of all, anger were boiling inside of me. I was standing here, looking in the face of a woman I called a friend. I had talked to her about the problems in my relationship, and she had betrayed me. *It's Jeff's?* Jenny was looking at me with tears running down her face and mouthing the words "I'm sorry." She was trying to voice her apologies, but I couldn't hear or think. I was in a complete fog. My memory was trying to recall the details that I missed when Jenny could have been sleeping with Jeff. I kept blinking at her in disbelief until I heard Mica's voice snap me back to reality.

"You are disgusting! A tramp!" Mica yelled.

"Please, Kamryn. I'm so sorry." Jenny sobbed.

"Please what? Don't you dare apologize for doing something what you knew was wrong! You have a whole husband and still want to sleep with someone else's!" Mica snapped.

"Mica . . ." I whispered softly, trying to find my voice to interject.

"You'd better be thankful you're pregnant because this could have ended badly for you today."

"Michelle." As much as I wanted to let Mica continue, I had to know. "How long have you been sleeping with him?"

Jenny sobbed even harder into her scarf that she was now using as a tissue.

"I wanted to stop . . ."

"How long?!" I yelled.

"Seven months."

"Seven months? So, because your relationship was falling apart, you had to go and ruin someone else's?" Mica chimed back in.

"I don't believe this. You've been sleeping with Jeff? When? How, Jenny? You're married to his boss, for God's sake!" By this time, a few mall shoppers had slowed down to see what all the ruckus was about.

"It happened before the holidays." Jenny's excessive crying was starting to get on my nerves.

"Just spill it, troll, and be specific." Apparently, Mica's, too.

"Jeff stopped by the house one day while David was out of town. He needed to drop off some checks that David wanted me to deposit into our account. I offered to come to the office; Jeff said he was already out and didn't mind stopping by." She paused to look down at her hands before continuing. "I had been so lonely. I was already drinking, so I offered him a drink, and somehow—"

"One thing led to another, right?! You people always use the same excuse!" Mica yelled.

"So, you've been screwing him in your own home?! Are you kidding me?!" I yelled.

"Kamryn, I promise I didn't mean for it to continue."

"Where else?" I asked.

Jenny was bawling now. Her scarf looked completely soaked, and her eyes were bloodshot red.

"The office and a few hotels."

"Did you sleep with him in my house?" I felt the rage spilling into my veins.

"No, of course not. I've never been to your home. I refused to go there."

"Oh, so, *now* you have morals because you refused to sleep with him in their home! You have some nerve!" Mica barked.

135

"I felt terrible after it happened, and I wanted to tell you, but I was scared of losing David at the time. Jeff convinced me not to say anything, and then, when it continued, I knew I couldn't. I fell in love with him. He said that sometimes, two unhappy people find love in unexpected ways."

"You felt sorry after the first time but decided to keep doing it for seven months? Yeah, that's believable," Mica stated.

"*Love?*" That word stung. "You love him?"

Jenny just nodded while sobbing uncontrollably.

"And he said he loves you?" I continued to ask.

Jenny nodded again to confirm. "It was unexpected, Kamryn."

My eyes started to burn, and my stomach began to ache. I was going to be sick. Not only had Jeff been screwing his boss's wife, but he had also gotten her pregnant and fallen in love. The pure thought of it all was more than I could bear. Jenny had been a person I trusted with my secrets. But more importantly, Jeff had been the man that I loved more than anything. This was the ultimate betrayal.

"Well, I hope you got what you wanted. You couldn't get a baby out of David, so you had to crawl into my bed. You two deserve each other."

"David doesn't know. But I know he won't forgive this. That's why I have to leave and start over."

"Good! I hope he leaves your sorry ass and beats the hell out of Jeff!" Mica yelled.

"You're not getting any sympathy from me. David deserves better than this," I chimed in.

"You have no idea what it's like, being stuck in the house by yourself while your husband is always away doing God knows what. Do you know he had a vasectomy just to make sure he couldn't have kids with me?!"

"And where do you think Jeff was?! When he should have been home with me, he was probably out screwing you! And by the way, I would get a refund on that love crap he sold you because you're not the only one. Ask him about Emi.?"

"Who's Emi?" Mica asked.

"That's the name of the other woman Jeff is about to have a baby with. The one I found out about."

I had never spoken that name again out loud ever since I had confronted Jeff—not even to Michelle, Lauren or Nicole when I told them he was cheating. I felt that if I said the name out loud, I would give it life, and it would all be real. Deep down, I still wanted it to not be true. But now, I wanted her to know. I wanted someone else to finally feel the pain that I had felt for the past few weeks.

"I am Emi," Jenny stated.

"What?" I asked in confusion.

"It's short for Emmeline. Jennifer Emmeline Lancaster."

This is it. This is going to be the thing that kills me. I took a step back to process what I just heard. Jenny was Emi. Jenny and Jeff were the "we." How could I have not seen this before? I glanced down at Jenny's hands—no ring. But she wore an emerald green, diamond halo necklace around her neck. Probably a set. Jenny loved emerald green diamonds. She told me once that if she was ever married to the heir of Diamond Rose Industries, that's all she would ever wear. I I cried the whole way home

t was a joke, though, right? Have I ever told her that Jeff's father owns Diamond Rose Industries? I didn't recall it ever coming up in conversation between us. Emmeline. Jennifer Emmeline Lancaster. The initials on the wallet, J.E.L. She was the one. The one who had ruined what was left of my relationship.

"Did he buy you the wallet?" I asked, suddenly snapping back into reality.

"What?" Mica looked at me and back at Jenny. "You've got to be kidding me."

"Yes," Jenny answered flatly.

"OMG. Classic monogram Jeff. Kam, let's go, before I lose my cool in this mall." Mica tugged my arm.

I could tell by Jenny's response that she was done feeling sorry; done feeling bad for the pain that she caused. She had done what she came here to do: confess. Get everything off her chest. And now, she was going to divorce her husband and walk off into the sunset with her baby and Jeff. The "we" could now be.

"You know, I feel sorry for you. And I hope you get everything that you deserve. You think you're going to be happy in this new life while you've created so much misery in mine?"

"I didn't mean for any of this to happen. I promise. But we're in love, and we're going to be a family." Jenny held her head a little higher this time.

"Well, I suggest you name your child Karma. Because it's definitely coming."

And with that, I walked off. I didn't want to hear anymore.

"Tramp." Mica had to get the last word in before running behind me.

*****

I cried the whole way home. Mica drove me to her house so I wouldn't have to face more questions from my mother. I texted my mom to let her know that I would be staying at Mica's tonight. She responded with a mind blown emoji, which was probably an accident, considering she didn't know how to use emojis that well.

I couldn't tell if Mica had been talking to me during the car ride, as I was so focused on my own thoughts. I did catch a few words, like *idiot* and *jerk*, occasionally. When we finally made it to her house, Mica moved around swiftly, gathering a pair of sweats, a T-shirt, a towel, and a washcloth for me while I cried on her couch.

"Can I get you anything?" she asked kindly.

"No. You've done enough."

"Are you sure? I could make us some margaritas strong enough to erase your memory for a few hours."

I could tell she was trying to make me laugh. We always relied on humor to lighten the mood in college, but this time, it didn't work.

"No, thanks. I still haven't recovered from last night."

"Okay. Well, if you need anything, just let me know." She sat down on the edge of the couch and rubbed my leg. "It'll be okay, Kamryn. Think of this as a purge of all the toxic people in your life."

"This is beyond toxic. This is just messed up. How could he do this to me? How could she?" The tears started falling again. I don't think they stopped since I left the mall. "I feel so stupid, and it hurts like hell. It's one thing when you don't know them. I could pretend they didn't exist. But she was a friend that I confided in."

"It may hurt for a while, Kam. But you'll get through this. And you're not stupid. He is, and so is she if she thinks they're going to run off into the sunset together. So, let the two fools have each other. You deserve better than him, Kam. You always have."

I tried my best to smile, but it fell short of anything sincere. Mica took that as a sign that I was done talking and went into her room. I was exhausted from crying and needed to clear my head. I wanted to think about anything but this. I reached for my phone to check my social media; nothing but happy couples, baby announcements, and the occasional scripture for spiritual uplifting.

I must have dozed off looking through pictures because I woke up to my phone buzzing on the floor, a sign that it fell out of my hand when I slept off. I reached for the phone to stop the noise and saw a text from Jeff pop up on my screen. I felt my heart rate instantly increase. Jenny probably told him about our little encounter earlier. Another text came in before I could even read the first.

Jeff: Jenny is lying. I am not the father of her child. It was a mistake, but you can't believe everything you hear.

Jeff: I can explain everything. We need to talk now. Please. I'll come to you.

I saw headlights appear in Michelle's front window, and I jumped up to run to the door. Jeff wouldn't be crazy enough to come over here, would he? I peered through the blinds to see a black sedan parking across the street. Not Jeff. I glanced up the street as far as I could see through the blinds, but I didn't see Jeff's car. Just a few cars parked on the street, which could be her neighbors. My phone chimed with another text.

Jeff: Kamryn, please. Let's work this out. I love you with all my heart.

Kamryn: You can't be serious. You get your boss's wife pregnant, who is also my FRIEND! And you want to work something out?

Jeff: I didn't get her pregnant! I told you; it was a lie. Please let me fix this.

Kamryn: Fuck off, Jeff . . . with all my heart.

I walked back to the couch and went back to scrolling through Instagram until I landed on a workout video from Charlie. It was of him and Ryan doing pull-ups in the gym. I watched the video a few times before clicking on Ryan's Instagram tag name. I wasn't following him, but his page was public, so I got to spy. He didn't have a lot of pictures; mainly gym videos and a few photos of him with family and what looked like business associates. Good Lord, this man is fine as hell. Every picture he took was a work of art. His smile, his style, and every inch of him was so effortlessly put together. I kept scrolling and accidentally liked a workout video from three months ago and I tried to unlike it quickly before he got the notification. I scrolled too fast and liked another picture of him with a little girl. Great. Now, I look like I'm stalking his page. I quickly closed the app and got up to go to the bathroom when my phone buzzed and chimed again. I checked, and it was an Instagram alert, a direct message from @Ryan_Ellis1.

@Ryan_Ellis1: You know lurking without a hello is an IG crime . . .

He is such an ass.

@KandiKam_: Since when is liking two pictures considered a crime?

@Ryan_Ellis1: Since you didn't say hello first.

@KandiKam_: Hi . . . Bye.

@Ryan_Ellis1: Hello . . . Leaving so soon?

@KandiKam_: Yeah. Not in the mood.

@Ryan_Ellis1: Sorry to hear. Everything okay? Anything I can help with?

Another alert popped up—a follower request from him. As I accepted his request, I wondered why we never followed each other on social media before.

@KandiKam_: Yeah. Can you beat someone up for me?

@Ryan_Ellis1: Depends on who my opponent is, but I'll gladly try.

I chuckled a little at his response.

@KandiKam_: Thanks. I'll keep that in mind if I ever need backup.

@Ryan_Ellis1: Backup? You sound like you're ready to go to war.

He had no idea.

@KandiKam_: Yeah, pretty much.

@Ryan_Ellis1: Are you sure you're, okay?

I didn't know how to respond to that. I was anything but okay. Frustrated, hurt, angry, embarrassed, overwhelmed with life, but definitely not okay.

@Ryan_Ellis1: Want to talk?

About ten seconds later, I was getting a video call from him on IG. Mr. Ellis was definitely proving to be persistent.

"Hello."

"Hey. How are you?"

"I'm okay."

"I don't buy that for a second. Plus, you look like you've been crying."

Shit. I forgot that I probably looked like crap. He, on the other hand, looked terrific. He was wearing a gray T-shirt and was moving around his house, holding the phone at a low angle, which allowed me to see his pectorals. I wondered what was on the bottom.

"It's been a long day," I responded flatly as I brushed my fingers through my hair and tried to clear the dry paste from my eyes.

"Who's the target?" he asked, now holding the phone directly to his face.

I paused. "No one. It's not important."

"You sure about that?" His persistence shone through again.

"Did you call just to get in my business?" My attempt to swiftly change the subject.

"No, I called because you seemed like something was troubling you."

"It's nothing."

"It's something."

"Maybe I don't want to talk about it with you." I regretted my harsh tone as soon as the words left my mouth.

He paused and glared at me through the phone. Not angrily; more out of curiosity.

"Do you want to grab a drink?"

"A drink? No."

"Yeah, I think you do."

"No, I don't. And it's late."

"What are you, eighty? It's barely 11:00." He chuckled.

I glanced at the cable clock and saw that it was 10:47 p.m.

"So, are you coming out for a drink, Grandma, or do I have to beg some more?"

"I'm really not in the mood, Ryan. I would probably spoil your evening."

"I highly doubt that. So, can I come pick you up?"

I rolled my eyes, and, to my surprise, he only smiled back at me.

"Fine. I'm at Michelle's house, so I can just meet you. Where do you want to go?"

"It's a surprise. And I'll come pick you up. How long do you need to get ready?

"That's not necessary. I can dri—"

"Gentlemen duties, remember?"

I rolled my eyes again.

"Has anyone ever told you that they can get stuck like that?

"Not since I was five."

"Hmm. Thirty minutes, okay?"

"Sure. Let me throw something on."

"Looking forward to it." He smiled before hanging up.

I got up to go check on Mica. I didn't want to disturb her if she was sleeping, so I knocked as quietly as possible on her bedroom door.

"Come in!" she yelled.

"Hey. I thought you might have been asleep."

"Nope, just watching TV. How are you feeling?"

I shrugged my shoulders. "I'm okay. I think I'm about to go on a date with Ryan."

Mica sat straight up in her bed and turned the TV off.

"What?!"

"Yeah. He called me on IG after I liked two of his pictures."

"Hmm, late night prowler?" Mica laughed.

"Shut up."

"So, spill it. What did he say?"

"Nothing, really. He asked me what was wrong and if I wanted to talk. I said no, and then he asked if we could meet up for a drink."

"And you agreed?" Mica asked, clearly in shock.

"No, but he persisted, and now, he's coming here in thirty minutes."

"Oh, I think I like him. Direct, tenacious, and persuasive enough to get you to come out of the house after the day you've had? Yeah, I like him."

"Well, I told him I was in a funky mood, but that clearly didn't matter."

"Good. I'm glad. You need this, Kamryn."

"Yeah, well, I look a mess, and I don't have a change of clothes."

"Well, first, go wash your face and moisturize. I'll find you something to go with those jeans and maybe a blouse."

"You know I can't fit any of your tops."

"Yeah, that's the point. They'll give you the perfect amount of spillage." Mica winked.

Mica was petite. We could wear the same size if the material stretched. But anything that fit her well usually squeezed every one of my curves.

"I'm not trying to look like a skank."

"Where are you guys going?"

"I don't know. He said it was a surprise."

"Oh, yes! And I have the perfect top. Go wash the tears out of your eyes."

"Ugh. I'm not in the mood for this," I mumbled as I stomped towards the bathroom again.

CHAPTER 13
First Dates

I thought about Kamryn almost every day after seeing her at Club NOVA, and then again at Michelle's house. Now, I was picking her up for an impromptu date night. I probably shouldn't even call it a date, since she clearly looked like she'd rather be left alone when we spoke a little while ago. But something inside pushed me to ask her out, anyway. Probably bad timing, but it was too late now. I pulled up to Michelle's house, parked across the street, and hopped out the car. Crossing the street, I got a sense that someone was behind and turned around casually to scan the street. Nothing or no one in sight. I heard rustling in the bushes near where my car was parked and tried to focus my eyes in that direction. Nothing. I looked towards the yards of the neighbors. Nothing. Suddenly, a cat darted out from behind a bush. I realized that his heart was pounding a little and tried to shake off the fear that had crept up in his throat. I hate cats.

As I approached the front porch, Kamryn walked out the door.

"Hi."

That's all she said. One simple word, and I was already losing my senses. She looked gorgeous. She wore a red and white top that showed off a little of her stomach and a lot of her breasts with light blue jeans that had rips in the thighs and knees. She looked completely different from earlier. She was glowing.

"Hi. You look nice," I responded.

"Thank you. So do you."

I looked down at my outfit—blue jeans, white shirt, and white sneakers—feeling slightly uncomfortable now after seeing her. At least I threw on some cologne.

"Thanks."

"So, where are you taking me?" she asked as we walked to the car.

"I told you it was a surprise. Don't spoil it."

I walked her over to the passenger side and held the door open. The bushes rustled again, and Kamryn jumped and grabbed my arms.

"Don't worry. It's just the neighbor's cat running around." I could have sworn I heard another noise nearby but waved off the thought to avoid scaring Kamryn.

"I hate cats," she said.

I held on to a smile and closed the door behind her. We drove in silence for most of the ride. Admittedly, I was distracted by her thigh meat hanging out of her jeans. Between that, her cleavage, and her perfume, I couldn't focus on anything else but her. When we finally pulled up to the location, the valet approached the car. Kamryn was already opening the door before I could walk around the car.

"You're going to learn to stay put one day."

"Learn what?" she asked.

"To let a gentleman be a gentleman."

"Don't you get tired of that line?"

We walked into the hotel lobby, and I could sense Kamryn starting to tense up. I paused and turned to face her.

"What's wrong?"

"Did you seriously just bring me to a hotel?" She sounded irritated.

"Yes, I did. You okay with that?" I asked teasingly.

"Seriously?" She turned to walk away, but I managed to block her path quickly enough.

"Now, do you really think I'm that classless to bring you to a hotel room for our first date? There's a restaurant on the rooftop that serves good drinks and calamari."

Still hesitant, I could see her mind considering her next move. She looked around the lobby and back at me, biting the inside of her lip. Great. She's annoyed.

"Fine."

We continued to walk toward the elevators. This time, I grabbed her hand to prevent her from walking away. She didn't hold my hand back, but she didn't fight me, either. We rode the elevator in silence to the top. I glanced down at her a few times from the corner of my eye and caught an eyeful of cleavage. It was going to be difficult managing not to stare at those all night. Kamryn stared straight at the elevator doors without even blinking. Maybe her mood was worse than I thought. We stepped off the elevator and walked to the outside seating area for the restaurant. Buck, the maître d', looked up when he heard us approaching.

"Mr. Ellis, nice to see you again. Back so soon?" Buck greeted me.

"Hey, Buck. I brought my friend out for a drink. Is my table free?"

"Yes, of course, Mr. Ellis. Right this way." Buck turned on his heel to escort us to our table.

We walk over to a table towards the rear of the roof, secluded enough for privacy but open enough to take in the view of the city.

"Can I get you anything to start off with?" Buck asked.

"No, I think we're good. We'll just take a look at the menu. Thanks, Buck."

"No problem. Just let me know if I can help with anything." And with that, Buck turned on his heels and headed back to his post at the front entrance.

"Mr. Ellis? You must come here often." Kamryn asked.

"Yeah. I bring clients here sometimes."

"Clients or dates?" Kamryn smirked when she asked that question.

"Clients, mainly, but I have brought a date here before." I regretted being so honest once I said it.

"Very original, Mr. Ellis."

"If it bothers you, we can go somewhere else."

"No, it's fine. This isn't a date. We're just having a drink."

"Oh, it's not?" I asked.

"No. We're just hanging out." Kamryn peered at me from behind her menu.

The waitress came and took our orders, then left us with an awkward silence again. Kamryn looked out at the view of the city while I looked at the view in front of me.

"This is so beautiful," she said, still staring at the city.

"Yes, it is," I responded, only staring at her.

The waitress made her way back to the table with our drinks, and I offered to make a toast.

"Let's toast to us hanging out for the first time."

"We've hung out before, Ryan. We've known each other for a few years now," she reminded me.

"Okay. Then, let's toast to our first date."

"Hmm . . . Very smooth, Mr. Ellis. This isn't a date," she said with a smirk.

"Well, it's the first time we've hung out alone, right?

"Yeah, but there was no need to before. I was in a relationship."

I could hear the change in her voice as she looked away.

"Well, let's toast to you not being in a relationship anymore, which allows for us to hang out alone. But not on a date."

Kamryn looked back at me and smiled. She grabbed her glass and took a sip of her martini.

"What's on your mind?" I asked.

"Trust me, you don't want to know." She took another sip of her drink.

"Try me." I took a slow sip of my bourbon and looked her dead in the eyes. After a long pause and deep breath, she finally spoke.

"I found out Jeff cheated . . . again."

"I'm sorry to hear that." I really wasn't, but I didn't want to be rude. From what I heard and observed, Jeff was very friendly with the ladies. "I'm assuming that's why you two broke up?"

"Yeah. That, and he got her pregnant."

"Wow." The scumbag didn't even have the courtesy to cover it up.

"I found out today that she was a friend of mine. His boss's wife."

I choked and almost spit out my drink. "Damn. Are you serious?"

"Very. She told me today."

"Wow. Kamryn, I'm really sorry you had to go through all of that. How are you dealing with the news?" I asked, shocked by what she just told me. This was the type of drama my mom and aunts talked about from their talk shows. I didn't think this stuff happened in real life, especially to people I knew.

"I don't know. I was just beginning to deal with the breakup. And now, to hear this, it's just . . ."

She broke off her words and looked back toward the view.

"It's devastating." She turned back to me, and I saw her eyes water. I wanted to hold her, just touch her in any way to help ease her pain, but I didn't want to cross any lines. She was vulnerable and upset. I put my hand on top of hers on the table and rubbed the back of her palm with my thumb.

"I can't stop thinking about all the times he was lying to me so he could be with her. Or the times she was smiling in my face, knowing she was sleeping with him behind my back."

I continued to hold her hand, hoping it would soothe her in some way. The tears started to fall, so I didn't want to interrupt. She needed to get this out, whether she wanted to or not.

"I feel so stupid." She continued, "How could I be so stupid all these years? I kept forgiving him, like I was waiting for more. I didn't think it could get worse than before, but this . . . this is unforgivable. We all hung out together—dinners, holidays, everything."

"You shouldn't feel stupid; you're far from it."

"Yeah, right." She gave a partial laugh.

"I'm serious. You're a lot of things, Kamryn, and stupid is not one of them."

Just then, the waitress walked over with another martini for Kamryn. Buck always kept his eye on when drinks were running low at the table, so I'm sure he sent her over. Kamryn pulled her hand back, took a sip from her glass, and looked around the restaurant and then back toward the view, obviously avoiding eye contact with me.

A few minutes later, our food came out, and we started our feast. We ate in silence for most of the meal, with the occasional moan from her when she was tasting her food. I had heard that moan before, and from the feeling in my groin, so had *he*. She looked so attractive while she was tasting, humming, and dancing as she maneuvered from her appetizer to entrée, then back to her drink.

"So, what am I?" she asked unexpectedly. I was so busy stuffing my own face that I hadn't noticed she stopped eating and was staring at me.

"Excuse me?" I quickly tried to swallow my food and wipe my mouth before steak bits started falling out.

"You said I am a lot of things. So, what are they?"

"Since when did you become interested in my opinion?"

"Stop stalling, Mr. Ellis." She folded her arms across her chest, pushing more cleavage to the top. Her breasts looked like silky, round melons. Admiring her face, I could tell she didn't have any makeup on, but her skin was still flawless and beautiful. She tilted her head slightly and blinked a few times to let me know that I was taking too long to respond.

"Well, I think you're beautiful, for one. Loyal, dedicated, ambitious, compassionate, kind, and resilient."

She sat in silence for a few seconds, pondering my words.

"And you can tell all of this from watching me tonight?"

"Who said I only started watching you tonight?"

"Well, when did you start watching?"

I opened my mouth to respond and hesitated to avoid making a fool of myself. Now is probably not the best time to tell her that I've always wanted her. But she had been forbidden fruit.

"I've always noticed you, Kamryn. We have mutual friends, so it's hard not to notice you."

"Noticing and watching are two different things, Mr. Ellis."

"Let's just say I did a little bit of both. "

"Oh, so, like a stalker?" she said with a raised brow.

"If you mean the way you stalked my page tonight, then yes," I responded with a smirk.

She tilted her head back and laughed.

"No, Mr. Ellis. I think you have that all wrong. I glanced at your page and accidentally liked a picture, and then you stalked me to go out with you."

"And look where we are now." I raised my glass to hers again in a silent toast to the evening.

For the rest of the evening, we talked about work, our friends, and a few embarrassing moments from our childhoods. She declined dessert because she was on a new diet regime that limited her sweets intake. I resisted the urge to tell her that she looked perfect and didn't need a diet and just asked for the check. As we walked through the hotel lobby, I could sense that she was calmer and more relaxed. I didn't have to hold her hand to keep her close to me; instead, we walked side by side as we talked.

The valet arrived with my car, and I noticed that she didn't reach for the door. As I opened her door, she looked at me with a slow grin and whispered, "I'm learning," as she got into the car.

"Happy to hear." I smiled back.

The drive back was different than the drive coming out. We were talking so much that I missed the exit and had to circle back around. Kamryn teased me that I did it on purpose, which I admitted that I probably did.

"They must be giving away Impalas at the dealership," I spoke.

"Huh?"

"Chevrolet Impalas. That's the third time I've seen one tonight since I picked you up."

"We're in the high tourist season, and those are popular. I used to rent them all the time in college."

"You took a lot of road trips?" I asked.

"Only a few. We would rent them to go visit family, take road trips, or go to the shore for a weekend."

"We?" Ryan inquired.

"Sometimes, it was me and Jeff; other times, it was me and the girls."

We pulled up to Michelle's house a few minutes later. I didn't try to kiss her or hold her hand out of fear of rejection and her thinking I was moving too fast. Besides, she said this wasn't a date, more so a casual outing between friends. We said our goodbyes while keeping a fair amount of space between us—intentionally on my end. I waited for her to close the door before I turned around and headed back to my car. I got in and checked my mirrors, and right as I pulled off, I spotted it: Another black Chevy Impala.

CHAPTER 14
Private Eye

———⌁———

How dare she? How fucking dare she? That's all Jeff could think as he sat in his car. He drove over to Mica's house to try and talk it out with her and smooth things over, but now, he had other plans. She was with someone else. Has she been with him this whole time? They had only broken up a few weeks ago, and it appeared she was already dating. Not some new guy—it was someone he knew. Someone he shook hands with and shared words with. Now, this jerk was trying to take what was his. This had to be going on while they were together, and Jeff planned to have a few words with Kamryn about it. She would have to explain why she would leave him for cheating when she had clearly been doing the same thing.

He had watched as Kamryn came out of the house and got into the car, seemingly comfortable. She had obviously been with him before. They pulled off, and Jeff couldn't help but to follow. The location finder he had on Kamryn's phone led him to Michelle's house tonight. He hadn't intended on following her; he just wanted to talk to her but lost his nerve when he saw her come out of the house. He had half of the mind to get out of the car and force Kamryn to come back home with him, but first, he had to get to the bottom of this guy she was seeing. He couldn't remember his name but knew he was a part of their little circle of friends.

Jeff tried to keep as much distance as possible to avoid being seen, but he needed to stay close on their tail. He knew Kamryn wouldn't notice him. His car was in the shop, so he had been driving around in a rental for a few days. As their car slowed down and signaled into the parking lot of a hotel, Jeff pulled into the parking lot of the mini mall across the street and quickly turned off the headlights to avoid attention. He was only able to catch a glimpse of them for a few seconds as they entered the hotel, so he decided to wait.

He couldn't believe Kamryn would cheat on him, but it was obvious she had an ulterior motive for leaving him. He decided to do some digging while he waited for them to exit, no matter how long it took. It only took a few minutes to find him on Michelle's boyfriend, Charles's, page. Ryan Ellis. They didn't have any photos together, but he was clearly a gym buff. After a few Google searches, Jeff found that Ryan was the owner of several gyms and various other local businesses and an investor of some sorts. Surprisingly, he'd never heard of him before in his own investment circles, so he must have only local dealings. No kids, no steady woman on his arm, and no recent family photos.

Everything about this guy, other than a few business articles, was a complete mystery.

Jeff checked his watch—12:37 a.m. It's not like her to stay out extremely late, so they must have plans to stay the night. His blood began to boil at the thought of Kamryn being with another man. He decided to go inside and see if he could get their room number. As he approached the front desk, Jeff scanned the hotel lobby, which was fancier than expected from the outside. The exterior was more rustic, but the interior was upscale and modern.

"Good evening, sir. Are you looking for a room?" the receptionist asked.

"No, thanks. I wanted to check in on my brother. Can you tell me what room he's in? Ryan Ellis."

"Unfortunately, we're not allowed to give out guest information. Maybe you can call your brother, and he can provide the details you need."

"I tried, but the phone is dead."

"I'm sorry, sir." She seemed friendly but conflicted about being able to help.

"Can you just check if he has a room here? I've been looking for him all night. He's going through a bad breakup. His wife left him."

She paused. Women tend to love the idea of a heartbroken man in need of emotional support.

"I promise I won't even go up. I just need to know that he's safe."

She smiled at my candor. Another trigger for women: sincerity.

"Sure. What was the name again?"

"Ryan Ellis. E-L-L-I-S."

"Ellis. I'm sorry; I don't see any guests here by that name."

"Okay. Thank you for your help, Miss." Jeff offered her a kind smile and turned to walk away.

"Theresa. And it was my pleasure. I hope you find your brother." She smiled back.

He paused. "Can I ask you for another favor? Do you mind checking under another name? There's a chance he may not want to be found, so I just want to be sure."

"Sure." Her mood was lighter now; she was friendly and more eager to help. "What's the name?"

"Hanover. H-A-N-O-V-E-R."

"Hanover, Hanover . . . Nope. No guests by that name, either. I'm sorry."

"Thank you, Theresa. You've been very helpful." Jeff felt relieved that Kamryn's name didn't come up in the system. He was scared that he may not have been able to control his temper if it had.

Jeff walked back towards the front entrance before deciding to stop at the restaurant in the lobby and headed straight to the bar. He knew they were here, so he just had to wait them out. After two drinks, he realized he was hungry from being out all night. He waved the bartender over to get his attention.

"Another round?"

"Do you have a menu I can look at?"

"No, sir. The kitchen is closed for the evening."

"Great. Another whiskey, then." Jeff sucked his teeth in disgust.

"Sure." The bartender quickly made his third drink and placed his glass in front of him on a fresh napkin.

"Thanks." Jeff always appreciated for good service.

"There's a restaurant upstairs that stays open until 2:00 a.m., if you're interested. You might still be able to catch them and order something to go."

"Upstairs?" Jeff questioned.

"Yeah, on the rooftop. Blue Lagoon."

"Okay. Thanks."

Jeff checked his watch again—1:26 a.m. It was too risky to walk into the restaurant and risk being seen by them. No doubt, the place would be close to empty at this time of night right before closing, so he had to wait it out here. He sipped his drink and decided to move his seat to the end of the bar so he could get a better view of the elevator. Twenty minutes later, he spotted them exiting the elevator. He observed as they casually strolled through the lobby, exchanging chitchat and small glances. Jeff gripped his glass so hard; he was certain that it would shatter. He signaled for the bartender again.

"How much do I owe?" he asked as he pulled out his wallet.

"That'll be $51 even, sir."

Jeff pulled out a $100 bill and slid it across the bar. No time to pay with his card.

"Keep the change."

He headed towards the front door cautiously, making sure that they couldn't see him as he approached from behind. He heard the bartender yell, "Thank you!" behind him, but he was too busy to acknowledge him. As he reached the front entrance, he saw Ryan's taillights heading towards the parking lot exit. Once in the clear, he made a dash through the parking lot and across the street to the mini mall, avoiding being hit by oncoming traffic. He was going to have to break a few traffic laws to catch up and find out where this Ryan guy lived.

Jeff veered in and out of traffic, trying to catch up, not caring if they noticed him. Thankfully, the Impala windows were tinted enough that he could pull up right beside them and neither would know. He was almost right behind them until he got caught at a red light and had to stop. The sound of his breaks could have blown his cover, but Ryan and Kamryn cruised ahead in front of him. He pulled up the tracker on his phone again to see which direction they were headed. Based on the GPS, they seemed to be heading back towards Michelle's house. Jeff took a sigh of relief that Kamryn wouldn't be spending the night with this guy after all.

Green light. Jeff took off like the speed of light and headed toward the freeway. He knew the way to Michelle's house, so he took the liberty of speeding on the freeway so he could catch Kamryn before she went inside. He still wanted to talk to her but when Ryan wasn't there. If he was, even better. Ten minutes later, he was on Michelle's street. He searched around but didn't see Ryan's car, so maybe Kamryn was already inside. He checked the dashboard clock—2:19 a.m. Someone had taken the spot he was in earlier, so he had to circle the neighborhood again to find a spot. No luck.

As he approached Michelle's street again, he saw Ryan walking to his car, which was now in front of Michelle's driveway.

He slowed the car quickly in the middle of the street a few houses down. No sign of Kamryn. As Ryan approached the driver's side, Jeff had the sudden urge to take his foot off the break and plow full steam ahead. He didn't like the smile of contentment on his face. Ryan scanned the neighborhood as if he was searching for something, then got in the car. After he pulled off, Jeff checked the tracker again. Kamryn was inside. He opened his social media apps—no new pictures or stories on either of their pages.

He decided to call it a night and headed home. Ryan would be spared for the night.

CHAPTER 15
Proposal

————◦◦◦————

I pulled into an empty parking space of the new Willis Towers. I was meeting Nicole here at 1:00 p.m. to see a few vacancies. Unfortunately, I was running a few minutes behind and knew I would have hell to pay for it. Nicole was already standing out in front of the leasing office, tapping her foot and pointing to her watch.

"Let's go, girl. Time is money!" Nicole exclaimed.

"It's 1:07, Nic. Jeez Louise." I quickly hustled my steps to greet her.

"You're late."

"I know. I'm sorry. I couldn't get away for lunch. I only have thirty minutes before I have to start heading back."

"I can do a lot within thirty minutes. Let's go."

Nicole looped her arm in mine and brisked me away to look at apartments. As we hurried along, I took in as much as I could fill my eyes with. The location was really spectacular, with floor to ceiling windows, large closets, a washer and dryer in the unit, and, not to mention, a state-of-the-art kitchen. The views were more spectacular the higher up you went. Some units had city views for miles, while others had garden or pool views which were equally stunning.

Nicole showed me the third unit on the list, which had an ensuite in addition to the guest bathroom in the hall. I've always wanted a private bathroom, especially after living with Jeff. This unit was special because of the spacious patio and the view of the complex. I envisioned a lot of people watching from here.

"So, what do you think?" Nicole asked me while watching me from a distance.

"I think it looks expensive."

"Yes, it has a hefty price tag, which you can afford. But it offers an extra level of safety with twenty-four-hour security, an on-site gym, running paths, and parks, and it's central, so you'll be able to get everywhere within fifteen minutes. Hopefully, on time . . ." She chuckled as she mumbled the last part.

"Very funny."

"There's another villa I can show you with half of the amenities. It's in a decent area but doesn't have the twenty-four-hour security that you requested."

"Yeah, which I need."

"Why?" Nicole asked, more concerned.

I moved closer to the patio door and took in the bright views. Down below, a woman was pushing a stroller through the courtyard towards the park. I touched my own belly and wondered if a family would ever be possible for me.

"Kam?"

"Yeah?" Nicole's voice snapped me out of my trance.

"What's going on? Why do you think you need twenty-four-hour security?" She pressed.

"I don't know; maybe it's nothing. Jeff has been leaving me a ton of messages lately. He's been relentless about wanting to talk. Plus, Lauren said something to me the other day that gave me the creeps."

"What did she say?" Nicole was standing beside me now, facing me as I continued to stare through the glass doors.

"She said Jeff is dangerous, and I should stay away from him. She seemed . . . odd. Almost nervous to talk to me."

"Yeah, well, it is a delicate situation. That is her brother, so I can see how it can be uncomfortable for her. For both of you, honestly."

"Yeah, you're right."

"Do you think Jeff would do something to harm you?" she asked.

I opened my mouth to answer, and I hesitated to say what came to mind. Instead, I looked down at my hands and feet and nervously straightened my clothes.

"Kam, what is it? Has Jeff ever hurt you?"

"Only a few shoves here and there; nothing too serious."

"I would say that's pretty serious." Nicole's voice was growing more concerned.

"I don't feel he would do anything crazy. I think he's just shocked. I did leave without telling him, so I'm sure it was a surprise. Hell, I'm still surprised I left, too."

"You know, Kam, if you don't feel safe, you should go to the police."

"The police? No, that's not necessary. Jeff cares too much about his reputation to do anything that would jeopardize that. He wouldn't let anything affect his career."

"Anything except for sleeping with his boss's wife."

I looked at her for the first time in our conversation. I forgot I told Nicole about what happened.

"Sorry." She sounded remorseful.

"Don't be. You're right."

"Look, twenty-four-hour security is great, but it won't stop people from causing harm if that's what they intend on doing."

"It's not that. It's just a big step, you know?"

"What, getting your own place?" she inquired.

"No, moving on."

Nicole agreed to send over the paperwork later so I could take a final look at the numbers and compare the three units. Moving on suddenly felt like a bigger commitment than it had before. Somehow, deep down, I thought I would go back; that Jeff would be able to convince me to come home. I had forgiven and believed his stories countless times before. I thought back to all the times I suspected Jeff was cheating with women, who he had claimed that "she was just a friend". Turns out, Jeff had a lot of female friends and play cousins. Once in college, he used my computer in my dorm room in between classes to check his email. Later that night, Jeff's Facebook notifications popped up when I logged into my computer; astonishingly, he forgot to sign out. Out of curiosity and some lack of trust, I opened the notifications and went through a few messages. To my surprise, Jeff had been dating and sleeping with at least six other women on campus, some of whom I knew. I recognized one woman from my dorm. The others had smiled and waved in my face all semester or had classes with me.

When I confronted him, he swore that none of the other women meant anything to him, he was mostly playing around, and nothing sexual ever happened between them. And just like Boo

Boo the Fool, I believed him. Even then, I knew that I forgave him too soon because nothing changed.

A few months later, a girl that Jeff had claimed was a strictly platonic friend magically left her underwear in his apartment on the same night Jeff claimed to be out with his friends.

I asked, "Why would her underwear even be off in your apartment?"

He said, "Kamryn, I've told you she's a friend. Maybe she took a shower between classes and forgot them."

"So, she can't take showers in her room? Why does she need to do that over here?"

His response: "She's just a friend, babe. And when a friend asks to come over to use my bathroom, I don't ask any questions. Plenty of my friends have showered here."

"You must think I'm stupid, don't you?"

I guess I had been stupid. I walked back into the office and hurriedly rushed toward my desk. Margaret poked her head out of her office and summoned me to meet with her. I shoved my purse into the desk and quickly grabbed my notepad. I had only been here for a few weeks, and I was already getting in trouble. No more lunch trips; next time, I'll just eat in the lunchroom.

"Hi, Margaret. You wanted to speak with me?" I politely knocked on her open door.

175

"Yes; I was looking for you. Come in and close the door, please."

I walked in and sat in one of the comfy lounge chairs adjacent to her desk, wondering if I should lead with an apology for being a few minutes late back from lunch. Good thing I hadn't signed the papers for that apartment just yet.

"So, I have some good news for you. Ambi has accepted your design proposal as one of the top two finalists, with a few ideas that they would like us to incorporate. It's between you and Nolan, so I need your reiterations by next week so we can nail down one."

I sat in silence with my mouth hanging open for a few seconds before I realized that Margaret was waiting for me to respond.

"Uhhh . . . yes. Yes, I can do that." Not quite as articulate as I would have liked to be.

"Yes! I know, it's exciting." Margaret offered a comforting smile. "But this is only the beginning. Once a design is selected, it'll be full steam ahead on the project plan, and I would like you to take the lead with me. It'll be the quickest way to get you acclimated to the company."

"Yes, of course. Thank you," I responded, finally able to relocate my basic vocabulary.

"Don't thank me just yet. Get those reiterations to me by next week. I sent you an email with the client's vision and expectations. And feel free to partner with Nolan or someone else on the team. It's not a competition; we just want the best version for the client."

"Yes; will do. Thank you, again," I say, as I make my way back to my desk.

"Oh, and Kamryn, congratulations." Margaret gave me another reassuring smile before turning back to her computer and pounding on her keyboard. The rumor around the office is that you can hear her typing even with her office door closed and loud music playing.

Once at my desk, I hastily checked my email and started taking notes and mapping out new specifications for redesign. I was going to be working day and night on this in order to meet the new deadline. Just then, Nolan popped his head over to my desk.

"Hey! You heard the news?" he asked.

"Yeah, Margaret just filled me in. Congrats," I responded.

"Thanks. You, too. Kind of exciting, huh?"

"Yes, and scary, too," I admit.

"A few are meeting in the conference room at three to get a head start on the updates. Are you interested, or are you more of a solo roller?

"No, I'm definitely interested. Thanks for the heads up."

"Of course. See you in a bit."

3:00 quickly turned into 6:00 as we all sat around sharing design ideas on the screen. Even after two cups of coffee, I was starting to see double from exhaustion. Margaret and Sarah had already waved their goodbyes for the evening, so it was just the five of us left on the floor. By the time I made it to my desk, it was closer to 6:30 p.m. I left my phone at my desk to avoid distractions, so by now, I expected over a hundred messages in the group chat.

To my surprise, nothing from the girls—just Jeff and, to my delight, a message from Ryan. I contemplated deleting Jeff's messages but decided to simply ignore them for now and opened Ryan's message.

Ryan: Hey, stranger . . . Hope you're having a good week.

Simple and sweet, but it made me smile. Other than exchanging a few memes on Instagram, we hadn't spoken since we went out. Undeniably, I'd thought about him often since then, if often meant every single day.

"Hey. I'm heading home. I'm beat. Are you staying here much longer?" Nolan's question startled me, causing me to drop my phone on my desk.

"No, I'm actually right behind you," I said as I gathered my laptop, notepad, and phone into my bag.

My mind immediately went back to Ryan as we headed to the elevator. Nolan was talking, but my thoughts were on the last time I saw Ryan. Now, seeing his message, I desperately wanted to see him again. I reminded myself to text him back as soon I made it to the car.

CHAPTER 16
New place, who dis?

———⚜———

"Kamryn, what about this one?" Angela yelled from across the store as she lay back on a display sofa.

"It's nice, but I don't know if I want a sectional."

"Come sit and see if you like it," Angela stated.

I obliged my mother's request and sank into the sofa. It was comfortable, but it was too big—more for a family of four instead of a single woman.

"Comfy, isn't it?" she insisted after I didn't respond right away.

"Yes, it is. But it's kind of big, right? Maybe a little too large for the living room."

"You could downsize and have them remove one of the sections in the middle."

"Yeah, but I think I would prefer a few accent chairs and maybe one couch or loveseat."

"Okay. So, how about this one over here?"

My mother quickly hurried over to the next sofa. I was amazed at how she wasn't completely worn out by now. I, on the other hand, felt every bit of pain in my leg and back muscles.

"I don't think I like the color on this one," I said as I walked up to the couch my mother was fixated on.

"Check the tag and see what other color options they have."

"Nope. Only gray, green, and blue."

"And you want cream or beige, right?" she inquired.

"Yeah. I want to keep the space bright and let a lot of light in. We had a gray couch at Jeff's place, and it made the space feel dark and gloomy."

"Don't blame that on the couch, honey. That home never had good energy. The few times I was there, I couldn't wait to leave."

She was right. We rarely had visitors, which I blamed on the distance and the fact that Jeff wasn't a great host. He didn't enjoy having friends over and always preferred to go out rather than stay in. When we did try to entertain, there were frequent awkward moments and silent stares around the room. I pondered if everyone knew something I didn't all those years and just waited around for the pin to drop. My mother once joked that the home needed healing and lit sage smudge sticks the few times she visited, which didn't help.

We continued to stroll around the display room, going from room to room until something caught my eye: a cream linen and cotton blend couch. I rubbed my hands over the material and sat in the middle seat. Almost tempted to lay down, I sat back, placed my head on the back rest, and immediately felt at ease. I looked around at the rest of the pieces that I probably wouldn't need, but they were equally as elegant. I could almost replace the throw pillows with different designs to give the space and an extra pop of color. The color palette was bare enough that I could go bright, bold, or neutral. Now, I just needed to find the perfect accent chairs to compliment the space.

"Looks like we found a winner," my mother said as she sat down next to me.

"Yes, I really like this one. It feels sturdy and comfortable enough to take a nap on."

"Let's check how quickly we can get it delivered to your place. Hopefully, this one isn't on back order like the others."

After another thirty minutes of speaking with the sales rep and making delivery arrangements, I finally had a new couch. They promised delivery within two weeks, which was cutting it close to my housewarming, but I was willing to take the risk for this couch. I could always ask Mica, Nicole, and Natalie to push the housewarming party, which they insisted on throwing for me, back by another week. Mica refused to let me be a part of any of the decision-making. All I needed to provide her with was a list of names of people from work that I wanted to invite, and she took care of the rest. To their benefit, I didn't have a ton of names. But Mica did point out that I'd conveniently left Ryan off the list. It had been several long weeks since we went out. I admit that I was partly to blame for the lack of communication. He had reached out a few times, casually, and I was either too busy with work or apartment hunting, so I responded hours or days later. One could only assume that he had lost his interest by now, which was probably for the best.

"I'm so glad you found something you loved. God forbid, we had to go to another store," my mom stated as we walked to her car.

"I thought you were having a good time."

"Oh, I am, but you are one picky character." She laughed.

"You want me to drive?" I asked, sensing that she may have been tired after all.

"Sure, sweetie. I need to call your Aunt Pam on the way home, anyway."

I got in the driver's seat as my mom dialed up her twin sister to discuss the latest family news. I checked my mirrors as I backed out of the parking space, then suddenly slammed on the breaks, causing my mom to jerk in the seat and drop the phone.

"What in the world?! Did you almost hit something?" she exclaimed.

I stared into the rearview mirror, and then again into the driver's side mirror. There was a silver BMW with a driver inside, but I couldn't see a face. It could be him, but I didn't know for sure. I looked at the license plate, but it didn't help, since I never knew his plates by memory. The windows were tinted, so all I could see was a figure—no face, but the same build. I felt as if the person was watching me, staring right at me, but I couldn't tell. My heart was now racing. I could feel my palms getting sweaty on the steering wheel.

"Kamryn?! Are you okay?"

My mom's voice startled me, but I didn't take my eyes off the figure in the BMW. We were both waiting for each other to make the next move.

"Yeah, sorry." I finally answered. "I thought I left my phone in the store," I lied.

"Well, it's right here, you nut." She picked it up from the cup holders between us before setting back in safely. "Now, try not to kill us."

"Sorry, Mom."

She continued with her conversation with my aunt, and I slowly backed out of the space, far enough to get a closer look at the windshield of the car. It was still too dark to make out a face, but I could see a denim jacket on the body with a white shirt underneath. I shifted the car in drive and headed towards the exit and carefully watched my mirrors to see if the BMW would follow, but it remained in its parking space. I took a deep breath and proceeded to the highway, practicing my breathing while trying to calm my growing paranoia. We made a stop on the way to grab some food before we got home. I continued to check my mirrors the entire drive home, reminding myself there were more than one silver BMW owners in the area. I pulled into my mother's driveway, feeling a little more at ease, and grabbed the bags from the trunk as my mom opened the door. I heard some kids playing across the street and turned to wave at the neighbor but paused instantly.

Three houses down, across the street, I spotted it: the silver BMW

✶✶✶✶✶

Ryan tried to focus on running the last mile on the treadmill but found it hard to concentrate. It had been almost a month since he saw her, but somehow, she managed to flood his thoughts. They had barely been acquaintances for the last two years since Charlie fell in love with Michelle. He'd only seen her occasionally at parties or random events. And she only made it to half of those, which he figured was due to her relationship. He had only met Jeff

185

a few times, and he knew immediately he didn't like the guy. He was arrogant and stiff and didn't seem to fit Kamryn's personality at all. Kamryn was fun, sweet, lively, and, not to mention, drop-dead gorgeous. He never understood why she stayed tied down to that man for so long.

Ryan finished up his last mile and skipped the cool-down. He walked to the locker rooms, grabbed a towel, and was about to head to the shower when he heard his phone chime. A missed call and a text from Mica surprised him a little. He wondered if Charlie had gotten himself in trouble, which was highly unlikely, considering that he was head over heels in love with Michelle.

Mica: Hey, Ryan! I just called to let you know that Kamryn is having a little housewarming at her new place. I'm sure Charlie hasn't mentioned it to you like I asked . . . You know him, LOL. But if you're free and can make it, that'd be great! See you then!

Ryan put his phone back in his locker and headed towards the shower. He passed a mirror and caught his reflection, not realizing he had been smiling the whole time as he read Michelle's text. Was he really that excited to see Kamryn? Yes, he could admit that. Maybe it would've been better if she had texted him herself, but they weren't on that level he supposed. Realizing he had barely spoken to Kamryn in the past few weeks, he wondered if he was too anxious about seeing her. What if she hadn't thought of me at all—or didn't plan on inviting me, which is why Michelle was reaching out to me? He pondered through his thoughts of her while he finished showering and headed back into the locker room to change, smiling again. I'm going to see Kamryn tomorrow night.

Ryan finished getting dressed and debated putting his tie back on. It was close to 3:00 p.m., and he had wrapped up his meetings for the day, so there was no need to be in a tie anymore. He stationed a gym in the same building as his investment company, so he had a short trip back to his office. He took the elevator to the twenty-third floor, walking through the double glass doors leading to the waiting area. He approached the front desk and was pleased to see the office receptionist he hired last year, Samantha Hall. Luckily, this one was bright enough to keep conversation with him to a minimum, and he liked that—unlike his last receptionist, Rebecca, who was fresh out of college and couldn't keep her mouth shut. She kept telling everyone around the office she thought he was hot and how she wanted to sleep with him. He ignored the rumors for as long as he could until she stayed late one night and made an inappropriate pass at him.

Rebecca came into his office one evening after everyone had cleared out. He had been nose-deep in a business plan, reviewing it for a new development proposal in Westchester, when he heard someone knock on the door. Most of his staff made a habit of working long hours, so he knew now that she'd waited around.

When he heard Rebecca enter the room, he asked her if she needed anything and realized that had been a mistake. She lunged at him with her blouse open, reaching for his belt buckle. Ryan was able to swat her hand away and stand up quick enough, causing her to stumble and fall to the floor. He tried to help her up, but she was clearly embarrassed from his response, or lack thereof, and scurried away.

He told her firmly that this was unacceptable behavior and would not be tolerated in the office. Rebecca attempted to fasten the buttons on her blouse while making her way to the door. She was gone before he could say anything else. She never reported back to work. When people around the office started to question what happened to her, he thought it was best to stay quiet about the details but placed a formal complaint with HR so he could start his search for a new receptionist.

Ryan was very careful about the people he employed. He started his company with a few small investors and quickly learned that buying and reselling was his true passion. Ryan liked to keep his head down and operate from behind the scenes, so being a silent investor in new properties and existing businesses was a perfect knack for him. Turns out he had a propensity for picking land in prime locations and made his investors very rich in the process.

"Hey, Sam. Any messages?"

"Hi, Mr. Ellis. Yes, one message from Mr. Gordon Mason. He wanted to speak with you about a new business complex that's about to go on the market."

"Okay; thanks."

"Would you like me to get him on the line for you?"

"No, thanks. I can dial him. Just email me his number."

"Sure, Mr. Ellis."

Ryan was about to dial Gordon back when he realized that he never responded to Michelle's text to confirm he was attending. He pulled out his cell phone to text her back.

Ryan: Hey, Michelle . . . Thanks for reaching out. When and where?

Of course, he could make it. He had every intention of going to Kamryn's new place tomorrow, but he wanted to seem casual with Michelle. She texted back a few seconds later.

Michelle: I'll send you the evite with all the details.

Noticing he was a little anxious about seeing Kamryn again, Ryan tried to distract himself with work. He read through a few emails and checked his calendar for the next few days. He had one meeting tomorrow morning to inspect the foundation of a new housing complex before signing off. His phone lit up, and he saw a new message from Michelle. She had sent over the evite for the housewarming as promised. He looked over the details and saw that she was registered at Target. After adding most of the items he saw to his cart, he decided to just check out before he ordered everything off the list. He was always an impulsive buyer when it came to shopping for a romantic partner. Most of the items were little knick-knacks for the house, nothing too major. Modesty, a characteristic he not only admired but also respected. Ryan wanted to make a grand gesture to her someway without being noticeable to everyone else in the room. He was probably a little too impulsive because now, he had nothing to physically bring with him to her house. He opened the registry again to see if there was anything he could pick up in a store close by but was unsuccessful, so he would have to be creative.

CHAPTER 17
Foolish Me

I spent the whole day cleaning my new place and rearranging the furniture. The final building construction happened much quicker than I expected. Nicole called me a week after I signed the paperwork, stating that the apartment was ready for final viewing, and, of course, the place was still beautiful. After I had scored the perfect couch, my mom generously bought me a new bedroom set. Now, I was moved in and almost completely unpacked, thanks to Angela Hanover. She had everything set up nice and neat, meticulous as usual. I was getting ready for my guests later this afternoon. I swept up the last bit of dust I saw and stood back to view my new living room. The cream couch gave the room a sophisticated look, and overall, the room felt very welcoming, with neutral cream tones and touches of navy blue and gold to add some color. The accent chairs in the corner added a bit of spunk to the room, too.

The kitchen was smaller than the one I had shared with Jeff, but it had a built-in bar on the outside wall facing the living room, with four barstools also facing the living room. It was perfect for entertaining and extra seating. I gave Mica the green light to invite

Ryan since she was bringing Charlie after her incessant nagging on having the guys come, so there would be some more male testosterone. Not that I minded, I just hadn't seen Ryan since our last one-to-one interaction, and I was feeling a little anxious about seeing him this time. Thankfully, there would be other people around tonight to lighten the sexual tension between us.

Taking one last look around, I fluffed a few pillows on my couch and grabbed my Taboo and Boggle games from the hall closet. I'm a sucker for a game night, just like Mica. We used to have them all the time at my apartment in college. Jeff rarely came to those because even back then, he didn't like to socialize with my friends. After everything was set up and ready, I went to the bedroom to freshen up. I took a little longer than normal in the shower to release some tension. I decided to slip on some jeans and a semi-loose-fitting tank top. I checked the mirror and liked how the shirt was clinging to my breasts but draping nicely over my stomach. An image of Ryan flashed in my mind: He was running his hands over my body, admiring me in the mirror. The doorbell rang, snatching me away from my thoughts. I glanced at the clock—5:26 p.m. People were arriving, and I hadn't even started my makeup. I rushed to the front corridor to check the video intercom, Mica. I buzzed her in, unlocked the front door, and ran back to the room to finish getting ready. I heard Mica fumbling through the door with whatever she was carrying.

"Hey! This place looks amazing. I can't believe you're already moved in and fully furnished," Mica yelled as she made her way to the kitchen.

"I know. My mom really hooked me up with a lot of things I needed, so it ended up coming together quickly."

"It's so warm and cozy. I love it."

"I'm glad you're here early," I said, walking back towards the bedroom. "I just need to throw on some makeup, so I need you to answer the door."

"Makeup? Girl, who are you getting cute for? Did you invite a new man over here that I don't know about?" Mica gave me a questioning eye and smirk that told she already knew what I was up to.

"No, I just want to have a little makeup on, nothing special."

"Mm-hmm . . ." Mica gave me a side-eye and turned back into the kitchen. Knowing Mica, she was in there making a concoction that would surely have everyone passed out by the end of the night.

"Just answer the buzzer as people show up."

"Sure. Where's all the booze?"

"Everything's out by the bar and in the kitchen." I heard Mica shuffling around the cabinets until she found what she was looking for.

"Bingo!" Kamryn yelled.

As I was doing my makeup, I could hear Mica in the kitchen using the blender to mix drinks. The doorbell rang a few times, so I was sure I had a few guests by now, and Mica was surely passing out her deadly cocktails. I changed my clothes three times before doing my makeup and decided on the same blue jeans and tank top that I started with. I didn't want to look too dressed up, so I kept my makeup simple, as well. A little mascara, bronzer, and a nude pink lip would do the trick. I heard the doorbell ring again, and then a hearty laugh came from the front door, and I knew exactly who it belonged to. *Ryan.* My body must have known he was there, too, because I felt butterflies in my stomach and a sudden nervousness. I checked myself in the mirror one last time, blotted my lips, and walked into the living room.

I saw Ryan as soon as I walked in. He must have noticed me, too, because as soon as I entered, he stopped talking and stared at me. We made eye contact, and I nervously darted my eyes in another direction. I went around the room and greeted everyone one by one: Nicole; Natalie and her husband, Nick; Charlie; Steven; Denise; Bill (three of my old coworkers); Ryan; and

Lauren. I wanted to try and end this awkwardness between us due to my breakup with Jeff.

"Look who finally decided to join us," Lauren said with a little more than a hint of sarcasm.

"Hey . . . Good to see you, too," I responded. So much for ending the awkwardness.

"I can't believe what you've done with this place," Nicole said, looking around at the furnishing and décor.

"You can thank my mom for that. I think she should have been an interior designer rather than a nurse."

✶✶✶✶✶

As expected, Mica's drinks had everyone babbling all night about their exes and bad dates and making up their own drinking games. It was nearly 10:00, and the conversation had changed several times from work to TV shows and relationships throughout the night. Thankfully, no one directed their comments toward me or mentioned anything about Jeff. Lauren mentioned that she couldn't buy me anything she liked off my registry because all of the items had already been purchased. I noticed that, too, and had planned on calling Target when I got the email notification but got distracted by work. Who in the world would buy everything off the registry? It must have been a mistake. Jeff would usually try to flood me with gifts to apologize for his lies, but he didn't know I had a new place. Or did he? I was dreading calling him to find out. If it was him, every single item was going back.

Ryan and I exchanged a few glances throughout the night. We were on the same teams for Taboo—orchestrated by Mica and Nicole, of course—so we ended up sitting right next to each other. It was incredibly difficult to ignore his leg brushing against mine or his breath in my ear as he was trying to whisper game strategy. When our team won at Taboo, we jumped up screaming and gave each other a hug, in which Ryan's arms lingered around my waist a little too long.

"Kam, do you have any water? I feel a little warm," Lauren asked.

"Sure. I have bottles in the fridge. I can open the terrace door to let the breeze in."

I got up from the sofa to grab her a bottle of water and noticed she was following me into the kitchen. I took a deep breath to prepare for the overdue conversation.

"Here you go," I said, handing her a bottle of water.

"Thanks. Your place is nice." She leaned on the wall as she took small glances around the kitchen.

"Thanks. I really appreciate you coming over." I stopped, wondering if I should say more. "I know we haven't talked in a while. I was hoping this wouldn't affect our friendship, since . . .

196

you know." I didn't finish the rest of my sentence, hoping that Lauren would fill in the blanks in her head.

"I didn't think you wanted to talk to me about it. And I've been a little preoccupied lately."

"Yeah, Mica told me you had a stomach bug last month." Lauren looked down at the bottle of water in her hands but didn't respond.

"Everything okay?" I asked.

"Yeah." She paused. "Just a lot on my mind."

"Anything you want to talk about? You were always there for me when I came crying to you about my problems." I tried to force a smile to lighten the mood.

"Have you spoken to him recently?" Lauren asked.

"No," I responded and noticed she looked relieved by my response.

"Lucky for you. You don't have to deal with him anymore."

Lauren was never really fond of her brother, but there was something different about her tone. I couldn't tell if it was fear, disgust, or disappointment.

"Has he said anything to you?" I hesitated to ask.

Lauren made another awkward look, like she had something to say but just couldn't get it out. We stood in silence for about fifteen seconds that seemed more like fifteen minutes.

"No. We're not seeing eye to eye right now. You know, family stuff."

She shrugged, but I could tell there may be more going on than what she was willing to tell me. Jeff rarely had disagreements with his family because he hardly kept in touch. He was closest to his mother; that was even a stretch since the relationship had always been strained. What "family stuff" could possibly be causing dysfunction between a brother and sister who can barely stay in the same room for more than five minutes?

"At least you rebounded nicely." Lauren motioned her head towards the living room.

"Who?" I asked, a little surprised by her comment. But I could take a guess at who she was talking about.

"Ryan. Are you two dating yet?"

"No, definitely not. We're just friends, and barely that," I said as I watched Ryan engaged in conversation in the living room.

"Well, friends or not, he's hot, and I think he's got the hots for you."

As I continued watching him, Ryan was standing near the terrace door, talking to Charlie and Steven. He caught me staring at him and smiled in my direction. What is it with this man that he can always sense when I'm looking at him? I quickly looked away and tried to focus on putting some glasses in the sink.

"Well, you should consider it. Unless you're still hung up on my brother." Lauren made direct eye contact with me, as if waiting for me to acknowledge her statement.

When I didn't respond right away, she continued to ask again.

"Are you?" she inquired.

"No, but I must admit, even with everything that I know, it's still taking me some time to process that we're not together."

"Everything that you know?" Lauren asked suspiciously.

"Yeah. Too much to get into now, but let's just say your brother continues to surprise me."

"Yeah, tell me about it."

Her tone seemed sad and distant now. There was something going on, but now wasn't the time to press Lauren. I was just grateful that we were having a conversation.

"I think I'm going to get going. I'm feeling sleepy."

"Okay; no problem. I'm glad we had a chance to clear the air." I could tell she was lying, but I didn't say anything.

"Yeah. Me, too. Lunch next week?" she asked.

"Definitely."

I headed to the hall closet to get Lauren's coat and walked her to the front door. I thought it was strange that she decided to leave without saying goodbye, but I was going to ignore that for now. As I headed back into the living room, I heard the conversation heating up about people from reality TV and others who were caught cheating, a topic I currently hated.

"I don't understand why she's staying with him, and he clearly has a WHOLE girlfriend. Everyone knows it!" Natalie said.

"Because that's what y'all women do. Y'all love us and hate to leave us." Steven's response made my skin crawl, probably because he was right. At least, in my case, he was.

"Oh, please! You just said you didn't have a woman a moment ago, so clearly, no one is begging to stick by you," Nicole retorted, causing everyone to laugh.

"He does have a point. You don't see too many men sticking by women who did them wrong," Charlie chimed in.

Mica nudged Charlie in the side. "Shut it," was her only comment. I'm sure it was purely for my support and benefit.

"Thank you! That's all I'm saying. Know your worth, and keep it moving." Steven gave Charlie a bro pound for coming to the rescue.

"People just choose the wrong partner and try to make it work, knowing full well they need to run for the hills., Ryan spoke up.

"You got a point there, buddy." Nicole and Natalie gave each other a high five in agreement.

"Once someone screws you over, it's time to kick them to the curb. I'm team no second chances,*"* Ryan spoke up again, clearly inebriated.

"So, are you saying there should be no forgiveness in a relationship?" I don't know what possessed me to speak. Maybe it was the sound of Ryan's voice that was forcing my voice box to say things it normally wouldn't.

"I believe in forgiveness. But there's a thin line between forgiving and being a participant. If a person continues to show you who they are, why not believe them?" he responded.

"I guess you're a relationship guru, huh?" I asked.

"No. I just know what works and what doesn't. You knew Jeff was a prick years ago. It seems foolish to stay with someone who enjoys making a fool of you."

The room fell extremely silent, with everyone looking back and forth between me and Ryan. He had just insulted me and called me a fool in front of the entire room. I felt the tears forming in my eyes and fought to hold them back. My throat was tight with embarrassment and shame. Ryan and I were still looking at each other. I noticed Charlie covering his face as if he was watching a scary movie and Mica giving Ryan her famous evil eye. He must have noticed it, too, because he looked down at his empty cup.

"I guess you're right." I tried to swallow the lump that was forming in my throat and showcased my bravest face.

"Kamryn, I'm sorry. That didn't come out right," Ryan finally spoke when he looked up from his cup.

I excused myself and went into the bathroom in my bedroom. The further away from the living room, the better. I stood there, looking at myself in the mirror, replaying what Ryan had just said over and over in my head. Was it that obvious to everyone else that I was in a relationship with a man who didn't respect me? All those years, I thought if I pretended to be happy and in love, then other people would believe it, too. Now, I see I was the only one lying to myself. And of course, the person to make me realize that now was Ryan. Leave it to him to make a fool of me in front of people.

After a few minutes, I walked back into the living room to find some people picking up dishes and others getting ready to leave. Steven and Bill already had their coats on and were waiting to say bye to me before they left. Natalie and Nick had already left. I guess after the public display of my humiliation, everyone was in a haste to get out the door. It was for the best. I just wanted to be alone, so I was happy to see everyone go, especially Ryan, but he wasn't moving. He was still sitting where I left him, but

Charlie had moved to the couch to sit next to him. Ryan looked up at me from his conversation with Charlie, and I hurried into the kitchen, where Mica and Nicole were putting away leftover food from tonight.

"You okay?" Nicole asked first.

"Yeah, I'm good. Thanks for cleaning up."

"You want me to sock him in the eye?" Mica was always ready to defend a friend.

"No, but thanks. Why is he still here?"

"I don't know, but I can make him leave. Charlie and I are heading out now, anyway. Do you need anything?"

"No, I'm good. Y'all have done more than enough."

I watched Mica and Nicole head back into the living room and say their goodbyes. As everyone was gathering their things, I noticed Ryan was still lingering around. I moved around, picking up cups and going back and forth into the kitchen to avoid him until he was standing right in front of me. Ryan stopped in front of me as I was holding the door open and waving everyone off. For the first time since I've known him, he didn't look confident and composed.

"Kamryn, I'm so sor . . ." Ryan started to speak and offer an apology that I had no interest in hearing.

"Thanks for coming." I cut him off to prevent hearing his explanation. We had done enough talking for the night.

Ryan stood there for a few seconds as he was contemplating what to say next. Mica must have witnessed him trying to make nice because she subtly pushed him out the door in front of her as she was leaving.

"See you later, Kam. I'll call you when I get in."

After the last goodbye, I closed the door and locked up. I cleaned up the rest of the mess in my living room and put everything back to my liking, realizing that I may have a touch of OCD like I teased my mother about having. After half an hour, I knew I couldn't clean anything else. The place wasn't dirty, so I was mainly moving around to distract myself from feeling stupid and foolish. I went into the bedroom to undress and run the water for a shower. I took another ten minutes to take off my makeup and clean my face. Another one of my OCD moments—my morning and evening skincare routine.

I was just about to hop in the shower when I heard my doorbell ring. My bathroom door in my bedroom was open, so I stepped out to make sure I heard the bell. Who would be coming by tonight? No one even knows where I live. I grabbed my robe off my bed, put it on, and tied it tight, since I was fully naked. Whoever was at the door was about to be sorry.

CHAPTER 18
Mr. Obnoxious

Ryan sat in his car in front of his house for about ten minutes before deciding to drive back to Kamryn's place. He had to talk to her tonight and apologize for what he said. He tried to apologize before he left, but he could barely get the words out before she stopped and dismissed him. She was upset, as she should be. He could hardly believe he had publicly expressed his opinion about her relationship with Jeff that way. To make it worse, he said it in front of several other people. It wasn't his place or his style to butt into other people's business, especially relationships. He learned a long time ago that relationships were off limits, even if the people had broken up. There was always a small chance that they might get back together. And once you said something adverse about the couple, it was out there forever, lingering in the back of their minds. So, it was just best to stay quiet and let people figure it out for themselves.

He remembered the death looks Mica gave him across the room and the way Charlie was covering his face as if a bomb just went off. *What the hell was I thinking?* She didn't deserve that, and he didn't think she was a fool. He knew he was tipsy from those mixed drinks because he wasn't able to stop his lips from moving once he started. He was going to have to ask Mica what she put in those drinks once the smoke cleared and he wasn't at risk for being punched in the face. He knew he shouldn't be driving, and he normally didn't if he had indulged in alcohol, but this had to be done tonight.

Seeing Kamryn's face tonight after he has disparaged her nearly crushed him. She looked as if someone had sucker punched her, and he had. He thought she was about to scream or cry but was thankful that she hadn't. Ryan had prepared himself for a battle or a verbal assault, but she only responded in agreement to his statement, which made him feel worse. She had accepted his criticism with such grace; that wounded him more than he could imagine. He tried to wait for her to be alone afterwards so he could apologize, but she was masterfully avoiding him. Mica nearly punched him in the groin on the way out the door. It was a subtle gesture, but he recognized the warning.

Ryan pulled into a gas station a few minutes away from Kamryn's house. He picked up a small coffee, Tylenol, and some flowers that were still fresh after being picked over. He couldn't go empty-handed.

Kamryn walked towards the front door, careful not to make any loud noises just in case she decided to ignore whoever was at her door. *Who the hell knows where I live yet, anyway?* she thought. She got close to the door and looked through the peephole. *Ryan.* She backed away from the door and contemplated whether she should open it or not.

"Kamryn?" Ryan knocked on the door now instead of ringing the doorbell.

Crap. He must have heard her hooves as she was walking to the door. Kamryn sucked her teeth and tied her robe tighter before unlocking the door. She opened the door a few inches, just enough so he could see her face, and blocked the doorway so he couldn't enter.

"What are you doing here?"

"Hey". Ryan almost lost his nerve when he saw Kamryn in the doorway. He was expecting the jeans and T-shirt he saw her in earlier, not this thin robe that hugged every inch of her body. That, combined with the way she looked at him, was enough to make him walk away and hide under a rock. He'd never felt so intimidated by someone, but with Kamryn, it was different.

"Did you forget something?" Kamryn asked, knowing full well he hadn't because she had just cleaned the whole place.

"No, but I wanted to talk to you. Can I come in?"

Kamryn continued to stare at Ryan, noticing he had one of his hands behind his back.

"What are you hiding?" Kamryn asked.

Ryan revealed the flowers he had hiding behind his back—white orchid lilies. Kamryn's stomach tingled at the sight of her favorite flowers.

"A piece offering." Ryan tilted his head at her and smiled a little.

That smile. It was enough to weaken any woman's knees—or some men, for that matter. Kamryn opened the door, moved out the way, and motioned for him to come in. As Ryan walked in, he stopped in front of her to hand Kamryn the flowers.

"Thank you. How did you know I liked orchids?"

"I pay attention," Ryan answered. He noticed a few wall decals around her house earlier—all flowers, but mostly orchid lilies.

While Kamryn went into the kitchen to look for a vase to put the flowers in, Ryan walked into the living room. He had to get his thoughts together so he could apologize the right way. Kamryn approached from behind him and placed the flower vase on the table.

"They're very pretty. Thank you." Her face was stern and unyielding to a smile.

"It was the least I could do. I want to apologize for what I said earlier. I had no right to say that, and I'm sincerely sorry."

Kamryn folded her arms across her chest and continued to stare at him.

"You came all the way back here to apologize?"

"Yes."

"Why?"

"It was important to me."

"Why?"

Ryan paused, unsure of what to say next.

"I was a jerk, and I obviously upset you. I don't know why I said that, but it wasn't my intention to hurt you, especially in front of your guests. So, I just wanted to apologize and make sure that you were okay."

"I'm fine." Of course, she wasn't fine.

"Are you sure?" Ryan took a step closer toward Kamryn to close the gap between them. Kamryn could feel her body starting to tingle as he approached her.

"Yes," Kamryn whispered, feeling less confident.

"Okay." He didn't believe her. He wanted to pry but knew better than to push a woman who was already upset.

"Well, can I have a hug to make sure?" Ryan cocked his head to the side and gave Kamryn a friendly smirk to ease some of the tension.

"No."

"Please? If I have to get on my knees and beg, I will," he said sincerely.

Kamryn hesitated, and then responded, "Whatever," as she rolled her eyes. He just had to remember to tell her how cute she was when she did that.

Ryan leaned in and wrapped both of his arms around her waist. They never really engaged in a real hug before, just polite gestures to appease the eyes who were always watching. This time, he squeezed her a little tighter and held her little longer.

Kamryn hugged him and counted to ten in her head to control her breathing. She could feel the imprint of his chest muscles on her breasts. He felt so powerful but managed to be so gentle when he hugged her.

Ryan continued to hold Kamryn as he leaned back to look down at her face. She looked up at him, and he noticed how bare and beautiful her face was. He'd never seen her at this closeness without makeup before. He could see the freckles on her face, which he had never noticed until now. She was truly beautiful.

"I really am sorry, Kamryn. I hope you can forgive me."

"Thanks. I appreciate your apology." She started to feel slightly uncomfortable with his arms around her still and tried to wiggle away.

"You're really beautiful."

"You can quit being so sweet, Ryan. I'm not one of your little bimbos."

"One of my *bimbos*? What are you talking about?" Ryan took a step back, releasing his grip from around her waist.

"I'm just saying, you can stop being so sweet and seductive, hugging me, and calling me pretty . . ."

"I said beautiful," Ryan answered, stopping her mid-sentence.

"Well, your apology and the flowers were enough."

"No, honestly, it's not. I offended you in front of everyone, and I feel like an ass. I just . . ."

"Yeah, you did, and yes, you are an ass. But it's fine. I guess that's just your way," Kamryn said sarcastically.

"What way is that?"

"The way in which you choose to offend people with your obnoxious and unnecessary commentary, or at least the way you respond to most things about me."

"Obnoxious? When have I ever said anything to offend you before today?"

Ryan thought back to when he saw Kamryn at Club NOVA. Not his finest moment.

"Every time you open your mouth, you say something obnoxious to me. If it isn't about my ex, it's about something else," Kamryn shot back.

"I just always thought you deserved better; that's all. Jeff was a jackass."

"And you thought it was necessary to say that in front of everyone tonight?"

"No." Ryan sighed. "That was a mistake."

"Yeah. The only mistake was me thinking you're somebody that you're not."

"What do you mean by that?" Ryan asked curiously.

"It doesn't matter. Look, it's late. You should go," she said as she attempted to turn towards the hall.

"Kamryn." He grabbed her hand slightly. "Do you know how frustrating it is to see you dealing with that nonsense? I wasn't trying to embarrass you; I was just frustrated and intoxicated. It's not like it was a secret the way he carried on. It's like everyone knew he was an ass except you." He said the last part with more emotion than he intended.

The second the words left his mouth, Ryan regretted it. Kamryn turned around and stormed towards the door. Ryan went after her and tried to grab her by the waist again, but she pulled away.

"Thanks for stopping by. You can go now." Kamryn unlocked the door and held it open, waiting for him to leave.

"Kamryn, wait . . . Please." Ryan reached for the door and closed it. He locked it and stood in front of it to prevent her from trying to open it again. "I didn't mean to raise my voice."

"Ryan, look. It's been a long night. I appreciate you stopping by, but . . ."

"I screwed up again and pissed you off." Ryan surprised Kamryn with his statement. "I know I was out of line, and I can clearly see how upset and uncomfortable I made you tonight. It wasn't my place."

"You're right. It wasn't."

"I know, and I apologize. I think you're a beautiful woman, and I was just a little tipsy tonight."

"Drunk fools usually speak the truth. Or am I the fool? Isn't that what you said?"

Ryan felt the punch to his gut without Kamryn ever having to make a move.

"I don't think you're a fool. I think you deserve better than him. He's the fool."

Ryan grabbed Kamryn's waist, pulling her in close. He couldn't help himself, and as soon as he touched her, he knew he didn't want to stop. He squeezed her tighter around her waist and inhaled the scent of her hair. Kamryn wrapped her arms around him, slightly grazing the back of his neck with her fingers. He started to rub her lower back, and he heard Kamryn exhale. She felt so good in his arms, so natural. He tilted his head lower, placed his lips on her neck, and kissed her softly, unsure of how she would respond. Kamryn's body immediately tensed when he kissed her neck. She opened her eyes and looked at him.

"What are you doing?" Kamryn asked softly.

Ryan looked at her and paused for a moment, unsure of what he was about to say, probably because he was unsure about what he was doing himself. He had fantasized about Kamryn for months and occasionally, over the years, thought about what it would feel like to be with her. But now, he wasn't so sure. She was vulnerable and wounded from a previous relationship and still upset with him. Now wasn't the right time. But when would it ever be right?

"I'm about to kiss you."

Half a statement, half a question. Ryan continued looking at her, waiting for a verbal objection or for her to back away; she did neither. Kamryn stared at him, stunned. She wanted to back away and tell him "No," but at that moment, her voice had suddenly disappeared. She could barely think with his hand on her waist, but when he kissed her neck, she nearly collapsed. Had it been that long since she felt a man's touch? Or was she just reacting this way to Ryan's touch?

He leaned into her face and let his lips rest on hers. Kamryn responded to his kiss openly. Her passion matched his as the kiss grew more intense. Ryan rubbed his hands all over her body and squeezed, amazed by how soft she felt. Kamryn moaned, pushing herself closer into him, causing Ryan to stumble back a little. He caught himself, only now realizing her strength. Most times, he was able to control the situation, but Kamryn had her own power and strength that was sexy as hell. Kamryn had never been the aggressive type during sex—at least, not with Jeff. She never felt the need to because Jeff was quick—quick about everything. He rarely took the time to kiss her before or during sex. If he had, he would know that kissing was the ultimate turn-on for her.

Kamryn began to undress Ryan, sliding her hands under his shirt to lift it and reveal his abs. Ryan grabbed her hands quickly, as his shirt was almost halfway off. He wanted her but wanted to make sure she knew what she was doing. Lust has a funny way of making you regret what you did the night before. He didn't want her to regret any of this, even if it was just for one night.

"Kamryn, do you know what you're doing?"

"Yes. I think so." Kamryn could barely hear her own voice. She couldn't believe how quickly she responded to his question, but the truth is, she was very sure. She wanted this. She wanted him.

"Are you sure?" Ryan asked, rubbing his thumb across her knuckles. He waited patiently for her to answer.

"Yes," she answered confidently. She leaned up to kiss him again, this time with more control and hunger than she had before. Ryan placed his arms back around her waist and grazed down to her butt. He cupped his hands under her butt and scooped her up, quickly wrapping her legs around his waist. Kamryn was so surprised that she let out a little yelp.

"Not here," he said.

Kamryn continued to kiss him as he carried her into her room. Once in the bedroom, Ryan stood Kamryn on her feet in front of the bed, never breaking the kiss. He reached for her robe, but Kamryn grabbed his hands and stopped him. Instead, she took off his shirt and slid her hands up and down his chest. She could probably do this all night and be content. Once she was satisfied with how his skin felt under her fingertips, she unbuckled his belt buckle, then unbuttoned and unzipped his jeans. She slid his jeans and boxers down over his butt at the same time, revealing the size of his groin. Her eyes widened as she stared at his length and thickness. Where in the world did that come from? She'd never noticed Ryan's size through his clothes before, or maybe she just wasn't paying close enough attention. He was huge. She placed her hands around him and slowly stroked him. Ryan felt vulnerable, standing there naked in front of a woman while she was covered, maybe for the first time in his life. But this was Kamryn. He closed his eyes and let Kamryn take control. She pushed him back towards the bed, forcing him to fall backwards and sit. Now standing in front of him, she began to untie the straps on her robe.

"No . . ." Ryan reached out and grabbed her hands. "Let me."

Ryan moved Kamryn's hands away and placed them at her sides. He loosened her robe, allowing it to fall open and reveal all her glory. He had envisioned what she looked like naked, but his fantasies and dreams didn't compare. Her skin was smooth, without a blemish in sight. He noticed a tattoo of flowers on her right hip and wondered how many others she had. It was big without being gaudy and still managed to be sexy. Her breasts looked like perfect, round melons with Hershey kisses planted perfectly in the center. He couldn't wait to taste them. Kamryn had a full body, with the right amount of fluffiness and curves in all the best places. Looking at her now, all he wanted to do was squeeze her. She looked like a cup of warm hot chocolate waiting for him to take a sip. His eyes grazed down to her hips and legs, which held the gateway to her warmth and made his mouth water.

Kamryn started to feel a little insecure watching Ryan stare at her. She started to remember that she wasn't what Ryan was used to. All the women she had seen him with were beautiful women with smaller frames. Realizing she might not be his cup of tea, she wrapped her arms in front of herself, placing her hands around her stomach.

"Don't do that. Don't try to hide any part of you." Ryan moved her hands and slid the robe off, revealing the fullness of her body. "My God, you are truly beautiful, Kamryn."

He pulled her towards him so she could step in between his legs. Ryan put one of her nipples in his mouth and began to suck on her breast. Kamryn moaned softly while closing her eyes and caressing the back of his head. Ryan continued to suck on her breasts, moving from one to another while squeezing her hips. There was so much he wanted to do to her body that he couldn't focus on one spot. As Kamryn enjoyed the sexual onslaught to her breasts, she felt her knees buckle and her insides getting warmer. She placed one knee on the bed next to Ryan's thigh so she could straddle him. Helping her up, Ryan grabbed her by her hips, sliding her down onto him, feeling her warmth as soon as she touched him.

Kamryn stopped and closed her eyes. He was too big for him to slide in all at once. She eased down on him a little at a time until he was all in. Ryan watched her and waited while she adjusted to his size, being careful not to rush her. He wanted to be patient and allow her to take him in at her own pace.

"Are you okay?" he asked.

Kamryn only nodded, as she was adjusting to the pain and pleasure of him being inside her. She kissed him to help ease some of the pain and began to move her hips in slow motion. Ryan closed his eyes and squeezed her, trying his hardest not to apply too much pressure. She felt unbelievable. He placed his head in her chest and pushed his hips upward to match her rhythm.

"Kamryn . . ."

Ryan moaned her name as she continued to ride him. She kissed his shoulders and worked her way up to his neck. She sucked on his neck and made him growl. She smiled at the sound he was making, knowing she was pleasing him. Kamryn gasped and let out a moan as she felt Ryan grow inside of her and increase his rhythm. Ryan felt himself about to lose control and tried to slow down. In all the fantasies he's had over Kamryn, he never imagined she would feel like this. Every inch of her body was soft, warm, and sweet enough to lick, not to mention her tenacity. Every time he tried to slow down their pace, she would increase the motion and pace of her hips. She was ferocious in the most delicate, sexual way. He leaned back on the bed to give her full control and watched her breasts bounce and bump into each other as she moved.

Kamryn's eyes were closed as she continued to roll her hips over Ryan's growing bulge. She felt his hands on her hips making his way up to her stomach. She opened her eyes to look at him and saw Ryan staring at her. He looked so delicious. He moaned in delight, and Kamryn bit her bottom lip and let her head roll back. She held her right breast in her hand and stuck her tongue out to lightly graze her nipple. At the sight of that, Ryan leaned back up, placed both hands on Kamryn's butt and pressed their bodies closer together as he increased the speed of his own body. He continued until he couldn't control himself any longer. He exploded and wrapped his arms around her body to brace himself. Kamryn climaxed on top of him and felt her body go limp.

Ryan lay back on the bed with Kamryn in his arms. He shifted their bodies towards the head of the bed and flipped her over so she could lie on her back. He was still hard as a rock inside of her. Kamryn's eyes looked hazy as she looked up at him. Ryan leaned down to kiss her face, starting with her cheeks, then her nose, and lastly, her lips. She looked exhausted, but he was ready for more of her already.

"Round two?" he asked in a husky voice.

Kamryn opened her eyes and smiled. "Absolutely."

She wrapped her legs around him. Ryan kissed her on the neck, and she moved her fingers up and down his back. He began moving his hips, thrusting himself in and out of her, then decided he wanted to taste her instead. He moved down her body slowly with his tongue, licking and biting, causing Kamryn to open her eyes. He took his time on her body, nibbling on her thighs and stomach before he kissed her on the lips of her warmth between her legs. Kamryn made a sharp hiss sound and tried to sit up. Ryan looked up at her, pausing over her warmth, letting his breath linger close enough to cause her to squirm. Their eyes locked, and he dove his tongue inside her, licking and tasting her sweetness. He watched her as she enjoyed him. Kamryn arched her back from the bed and tried to hold Ryan's head in place.

He reached up with his hand so he could play with her nipples as he continued to lick and suck on her below. Once she was about to climax, Ryan stopped and moved back up her body. He hovered over her and listened to her heavy breathing. While she was focused on him, he slid himself inside of her. Kamryn gasped. He showed no mercy, pounding into her warmth with long slow strokes. He continued this until Kamryn clenched onto him, squeezing his back and pressing him down into her body, her hips lifting off the bed to meet his every stroke. She screamed his name as she climaxed loudly. Ryan erupted inside of her and bit down softly on her shoulder to stifle his own scream.

Ryan lay there for a moment on top of her, not wanting to let her go. He rolled over to get under the cover and pulled Kamryn close to his chest, worried that she may be cold. Kamryn snuggled up next to him, still feeling his hardness against her body. Ryan wrapped his arm around her waist and rubbed her stomach. The last thing Kamryn felt was Ryan kiss her shoulder as she fell asleep.

CHAPTER 19
It's Nobody's Business
———————⌘———————

Ryan stirred in bed a few hours later with a cramp in his left arm. Without opening his eyes, he moved slightly and heard a soft yawn. Kamryn. Kamryn was still lying in the same spot next to him. He almost thought he had a wet dream until he looked at her and thought of them having sex and how great she felt. She must have been tired because she didn't move a muscle all night. He kissed her on her neck and noticed a mark on her shoulder. He tried to adjust his eyes in the dark to see but couldn't tell if it was a hickey or a bruise from when he bit her last night. He tugged his arm free from under Kamryn's head and slightly touched the mark on her neck, thinking he may have been too rough with her. She muttered under her breath and grimaced. Yup, it's definitely a bruise. Ryan sat up, pulled the covers back, and turned Kamryn towards him so he could search her body.

"What are you doing?"

"Checking for bruises."

Ryan looked and rubbed his hands over her breasts, stomach, and thighs. He saw another small mark on her hip where he had obviously been too rough with her.

"Bruises?" Kamryn whispered.

"I left a bruise on your neck." Ryan looked at her solemnly. "And on your hip."

"It's okay. I bruise easily. Come lay with me."

He looked up at Kamryn and saw the sheepish, sex-filled look in her eyes that he couldn't resist. He placed a light kiss on her thigh and moved up to lie next to her. She was still fully naked with the covers pulled away as she lay on her back. He didn't like to see bruises on her but couldn't resist kissing and nibbling on her body. As Kamryn closed her eyes and started to doze off again, Ryan started rubbing between her legs.

"I'm sorry."

"Mm-hmm . . . It's okay. I told you, I bruise easily," Kamryn said, trying to focus on his touch.

"I was too rough."

"No, you weren't."

"Are you okay?" Ryan took her hand and kissed her fingers.

"Don't worry. I can handle it."

"I'm not just talking about your body. How do you feel about what just happened?"

"I feel okay. I feel really good, actually."

"That's good to know.

"Ryan?"

"Yes."

"Do you mind if we keep this between us? "

"Okay," Ryan said hesitantly. "And by this, do you mean what happened tonight or what will happen in the future?"

"Future?" Kamryn looked puzzled.

"I don't want our first time to be our last time. "

"I believe our first time was already followed by our second," Kamryn said, smiling.

"Our third time will come fairly soon." Ryan gave a sly grin. "But I really mean tonight. I don't want it to be our only night."

Kamryn thought about what he said for a minute. She assumed that this would be a one-time fling, but Ryan was asking for something different. Ryan studied Kamryn's face as she pondered his questions. He had hoped he wasn't being too forward with her, but he knew he wanted to be with her again.

"Only if it stays between me and you," Kamryn responded.

"Okay." Ryan tried to refrain from smiling. He felt like a school kid who got his first kiss.

"And we keep it fun, nothing serious."

"Okay." Ryan contemplated for a second but decided not to say anything about her "Nothing serious" statement.

"And we have to be honest with each other. No lies."

"Okay."   .

"I'm serious."

"So am I. Our business, fun, and honesty. Understood." Ryan checked off her three requests with his fingers to assure her that he was listening. He would have agreed to anything to be with her again. These were easy.

"Okay. Good," she responded.

"I have a request of my own," Ryan stated.

"What's that?" she asked suspiciously.

"No sex with anyone else," Ryan said firmly.

"Is that a request you can afford to make?"

"Of course. Can you?"

"Ryan, I don't know what you've heard, but I don't have an issue with monogamy."

"Well, contrary to popular belief, I only sleep with one woman at a time. I don't double dip, and I prefer my partner not to, either."

Kamryn didn't know if she was happy that she might have Ryan all to herself or bothered that it would eventually come to an end. Somehow, his "one woman at a time" comment made her feel as if she was his pick of the month. She wondered how quickly he would move on from her once they were done having fun.

"Hey . . . What are you thinking?" Ryan nudged Kamryn with his hip.

She responded by just shaking her head.

He could tell she was deep in thought, probably reassessing their arrangement. He didn't want her to have any doubts. Ryan lifted Kamryn's face so he could look in her eyes and brushed her hair away from her face.

"Are you sure you want to do this?" He asked, probing her again.

Kamryn paused and rethought what they were agreeing to. She was sleeping with her best friend's boyfriend's best friend. This was bound to fail and become a big mess. How am I not supposed to tell Mica? Mica could see through her from another state. She enjoyed being with Ryan tonight but wondered if it was worth the hassle of lying and sneaking around.

"Talk to me, please." Ryan nudged her again. "I don't want you to have any doubts," Ryan continued.

"I have a few," Kamryn finally responded.

"Which are?" He saw Kamryn hesitant and pressed her. "We agreed to be honest."

"I just wonder if it's worth lying to people just so we can sleep together."

"We could always tell everyone. But if you want us to be a secret, we don't have a choice, beloved." Ryan kissed her forehead. "What else is on your mind?"

"That was it."

Ryan knew she was holding something else but decided not to push her anymore.

"Are you sleeping with someone else?" Ryan asked.

"What? No." Kamryn seemed shocked by the question.

"Not even your ex?" Ryan's tone was soft but firm.

"Definitely not."

"Do you feel that may be a problem for you?" Ryan asked.

"Sleeping with only one person? Who do you think I am?" Kamryn looked at Ryan, offended that he was questioning her.

"No, but you never responded to my request."

"It's not a problem for me. I don't sleep around. Just make sure you hold up your end of the deal," Kamryn stated.

"That won't be a problem for me at all. I already told you I do one at a time."

Kamryn rolled her eyes.

Ryan noticed Kamryn's mood change when he said that, as she looked away from him.

"I didn't mean it like that, Kamryn. I'm sorry. I only meant that I don't believe in cheating and sleeping with multiple people. I never did. When I am with you, I'm only with you in every aspect."

"It's fine," Kamryn said, still looking away.

"Look at me, please," Ryan asked, which she did reluctantly.

"You're not just another random woman I'm sleeping with. So, please don't think that. I don't sleep with nearly as many women as you think I do. And I haven't had sex in a while—well, a couple of hours now."

Kamryn smiled, feeling slightly reassured. "I guess that's good to hear."

"So, is it just us, our business, fun, and honesty?" Ryan asked.

"Yes."

"Good. Because I'm ready for round three."

Kamryn smiled and wrapped her legs around him as he moved on top of her. Ryan kissed her on the neck, and she moved her fingers up and down his back. He began moving his hips, allowing his groin to massage her heat, then decided he wanted to taste her instead. He moved down her body slowly with his tongue, licking and biting, causing Kamryn to open her eyes. He took his time on her body, nibbling on her thighs and stomach, before he kissed her on the lips of her warmth between her legs. Kamryn made a sharp hiss sound and tried to sit up. Ryan looked up at her, pausing over her warmth letting his breath linger close enough to cause her to squirm. Their eyes locked and he dove his tongue inside her, licking and tasting her sweetness. He watched her as she enjoyed him. Kamryn arched her back from the bed and tried to hold Ryan's head in place.

He reached up with his hand so he could play with her nipples as he continued to lick and suck on her below. Once she was about to climax, Ryan stopped and moved back up her body. He hovered over her and listened to her heavy breathing. While she was focused on him, he slid himself inside of her. Kamryn gasped. He showed no mercy, pounding into her warmth with long slow strokes. He continued this until Kamryn clenched onto him, squeezing his back and pressing him down into her body, her hips lifting off the bed to meet his every stroke. She screamed his name as she climaxed loudly. Ryan erupted inside of her and rested his head on her shoulder to stifle his own moan, trying not to bite her.

Ryan lay there for a moment on top of her not wanting to let her go. He rolled over to get under the cover and pulled Kamryn close to his chest, worried that she may be cold. Kamryn snuggled up next to him, still feeling his hardness against her body. Ryan wrapped his arm around her waist and rubbed her stomach. The last thing Kamryn felt was Ryan kiss her shoulder as she fell asleep.

CHAPTER 20
There's Someone Else

—⚬⌒⚬—

I pulled into a spot on the street adjacent to the coffee shop I she was meeting Lauren. I was running behind, so I lucked out by not having to circle the block. Market Street was always buzzing with people, given all the shops and boutiques that stretched for miles. I scanned the street, not sure of whom or what I was looking for. She didn't see Lauren's car—Hopefully, she's running a little late, too. Walking toward the coffee shop, I saw a couple holding hands and shopping bags in the other. Love. How cute! It almost made me sick to my stomach, but I neglected the urge to gag in front of them.

As soon as I walked into the shop, I realized I needed a drink more than coffee and was slightly disappointed by the smell of coffee beans brewing. I scanned the room for five seconds before I spotted Lauren at a four-seater table to the left.

"Hey, Lauren," I said as I made my way over through the maze of chairs and tables.

"Hey, Kam."

"I'm sorry it took so long for us to get together one to one. It's just been . . ." I tried to think of something honest to say.

"I get it. You don't have to explain." Lauren reached over and placed her hand on the table in front of me.

"Thanks. Does this place serve alcohol? I suddenly feel like I could use a drink."

"Nope, just the usual: coffee, espressos, teas, and hot chocolate." She motioned to her cup and held it in her hand.

"I'm surprised you picked this place. You sure you don't want to go somewhere to get a cocktail?"

"No. I'm cutting back."

The barista made her way over to our table to take my order. I ordered the only thing I ever drink from coffee shops: an iced French vanilla latte. The barista informed me that she would have to double check if they still had French vanilla, so I told her hazelnut or caramel would be a doable supplement. My sweet tooth also needed a fix.

"Since when? You finally got tired of the drunken escapades." I smiled.

"Kind of," she responded with less of a smile.

"So, how are you? How have things been?" I asked, quickly shifting the subject.

Lauren looked down at her coffee cup before answering.

"Things are okay. Not as expected, but okay."

"Yeah? Tell me about it. That should be the title of my life documentary."

"I thought things were looking up for you. New job, new place, and I thought you had a new guy on the horizon," Lauren inquired.

I instantly had a flashback to our night together. Completely unexpected, and exactly what I needed. That was just a few nights ago, and I had fantasized about him every day after.

"Job, yes; place, yes; but no new guy. We're friends, and he's in a relationship," I lied.

"I see. I was hoping you two would have sparked something," she responded.

"Why?" I asked out of curiosity.

She hesitated, then stated, "No reason. I just thought you could use a distraction from everything."

"Hmm. Yeah, well, that's not the kind of distraction I need right now. What about you? Weren't you dating some guy? Aaron, I think, right?"

"That didn't work out." Lauren shrugged casually.

"Why? You were so head over heels for him a couple months ago, showing us pictures. What happened?"

"I don't know. It was bound to happen sometime," Lauren spoke and gazed into her cup, stirring her spoon as she was replaying a moment in time.

"And why is that, if you both liked each other?"

"I was in love with someone else," she said nonchalantly.

"What?! Who?" I asked, a little louder than expected.

Lauren's eyes darted up from her cup at me and then around the room, almost as if she was in shock. She seemed more surprised by her comment than I was.

"It's nothing."

"Who is it?" I asked, now pressing her for information.

"No one. Just someone from years ago who I never got over."

I thought back through the years of our friendship and didn't recall Lauren ever having a serious guy that she was in love with. She dated occasionally, but nothing ever lasted more than a few months. Other than that, she was usually single. So, where did the mystery lover come from? And why had she been so secretive about it?

"That's strange," I said, easing back from my inquisition.

"What's strange?"

"That you had someone that you were in love with, and we knew nothing about it. I mean, you never mentioned anything."

"He's very private."

"So private that you can't share this with your closest friends?"

"It's nothing, really. Honestly, I'm not sure if we have a future, either."

"Why not?"

"We want different things." She paused. "Unfortunately for me, I realized that too late."

"Well, whoever it is, he seems pretty special if you've kept him hidden this long. But if you're not on the same page, it's best to clear that up now before you move forward."

I started thinking about Jenny wanting to have kids with David all these years and how her frustration with David's lack of compromise possibly led her into Jeff's arms . . .

"We were at one point . . . planning a future together, but now, I'm not so sure."

"What's changed?"

Lauren looked at me as if contemplating her next statement. I could tell she was still very reluctant to tell me anything about her mystery man.

"There's someone else."

"Someone else? You mean he's with someone, or *you* are?" I asked, more confused now than when the conversation first started.

"We've always been off and on, so there have been other people. I've dated, he's dated, but we've always come back together. But this time, he can't let go of her," she said, looking at her cup again.

"Lauren, take it from me: Being on the receiving end of someone who is cheating on you or not being honest is no fun. Unless all parties are aware of the rules, only one person ends up losing."

"You don't understand," she said, shaking her head.

"What don't I understand? You're dealing with a guy who is involved with another woman, who I assume has no knowledge of your off-and-on relationship. It seems like it's time for him to be honest with either you or her," I said, trying my best to offer comfort.

"That's easy for you to say, Kam. You've always had Jeff, and you could have had any other guy if you wanted to."

"*Easy?* You think it's easy being with someone who is practically chasing every woman who walks by him? I'd rather have one man who wants me and only me."

237

"They always want you, Kamryn," she said in a soft tone.

"You deserve to be happy, Lauren. My BS has nothing to do with your situation. I'm sorry if I'm being too harsh."

"I'm sorry. I shouldn't be complaining to you about my problems, anyway. I came here to check on you."

"Oh, please. I'd rather talk about anything else but me right now. Trust me, it'll just depress you even more."

"But are you okay? I saw Jeff, and he didn't look so hot."

"Good. At least he looks the way I feel inside."

Lauren sat silent for a moment. She was always a good listener anytime I bored her about my issues with her brother. She had talked me through some hard times and often suggested I leave him.

"Where did you see him?" I asked after a moment of awkward silence.

"Huh?" Lauren replied.

"You said you saw Jeff. Where did you see him?"

"Oh. Um, at our parents' house. Jeff was there when I stopped by."

Her voice trailed off as she was speaking to me, as if trying to recall the day. Jeff hardly ever visited his parents. It was his mom who usually stopped by unannounced or invited us out to dinner, but he never went by the house unless for special occasions.

"You know, some days, I'm great, and I feel like I did the right thing by leaving. Other days, I feel alone. But mostly, I feel stupid. He was sleeping with someone right under my nose, and I didn't see. Or I saw it and chose to ignore it."

"Are you over him?" she asked.

"I should be. But I still get so angry thinking about those texts. You know we've tried to start a family. I wanted to wait, but Jeff begged me for a baby. It almost happened once, and we were both happy. Then, I miscarried over and over. Now, I just can't believe he's about to start a family with someone else."

"He told you about the pregnancy?" she asked in a whisper. Another group came in, took the other two seats next to us, and moved the second small table two feet away. They were still close enough to hear every word.

"No, of course not. I saw it on his phone when she texted him. He was in the shower."

"Oh," Lauren responded, in deep thought.

"Wait. How did you know?" I asked, realizing I had only told Mica and Nat about Jenny's news. And Ryan, for that matter. But with all the uncomfortable distance between Lauren and me, I never had the chance.

"Huh?"

"How did you know about the pregnancy? Did Jeff tell you?"

"Yeah. He mentioned it had something to do with why y'all broke up."

"Humph . . . Figures." I folded my arms in disgust. "It had *everything* to do with why we broke up."

"I'm guessing he didn't tell you who?" she asked cautiously.

"No. She did a few weeks ago."

Lauren sat back in her chair, with obvious skepticism and questions going through her mind. I imagined this is the same face I made when Jenny broke the news to me in the mall. Standing there, trying to put all the pieces together between your own perception and what was now a reality.

"Hard to believe, I know. He was sleeping with my friend right under my nose," I said, breaking her train of thought.

"Wait. Who is she?"

"Jenny Lancaster."

"Lancaster? Isn't that his boss's . . ."

"Right . . . His boss's wife."

Lauren put her face in her hands and shook her head in disbelief.

"I can't believe this," she said as her voice started to crack.

"You and I both. But I'll be okay," I said, realizing that she may be taking the news harder than I expected.

Lauren pulled out her phone and glanced at the screen.

"Ugh. I'm sorry, Kamryn. I have to run. I have a doctor's appointment not too far from here."

"That's okay. You go ahead. I'll pay for this," I said, then the barista came.

"Thanks. Sorry I have to run out like this."

"It's no problem. Go. I'll call you sometime next week."

She paused as she gathered her purse. "I don't deserve to have a friend like you, Kamryn."

"You are just as good of a friend to me. Who else could listen to all the drama of my life?" I chuckled.

"Do you still love him?" she asked.

"Yeah, I guess I do. Love doesn't go away that easy. But love isn't enough to make me stay any longer."

"You deserve better, Kamryn. Don't get trapped like I did."

And with that, she got up from the table and left.

CHAPTER 21
Hello???

The next few weeks were pure bliss. Work had been thriving, and I was adapting well to my colleagues and getting used to the rhythm of the office. There was always a project or a client in need. And if an existing client didn't have an issue, a new client was seeking design updates. The days were going by fast, even though the hours were long. And in between meetings, I snuck in texts and calls from Ryan. We were practically inseparable during the day and most nights. I was growing quite fond of our meetups at his place or mine. I honestly enjoyed the privacy that the sneaking around had afforded us. No uncomfortable questions from friends, and no expectations to share details of our escapades. I was starting to feel like a version of myself that I hadn't known in years.

My coworkers often caught me smiling at my desk or in meetings. They didn't say much, just nudged me if I seemed to be distracted in my thoughts. Ryan definitely had that effect. If he wasn't on my mind, then I was yearning to see him. The days we hadn't seen each other had become difficult, not because I couldn't go a day without him, but I had become used to his touch, his warmth, and his presence in the bed next to me. On the nights he wasn't there, I had to shift some of the pillows in my bed to make a fake mold to hold onto.

Just then, my office phone rang, breaking me away from my thoughts. *Ryan.* Only a few people had this number, and he was one of them. I answered quickly after one ring.

"Kamryn Hanover."

"Kam Kam . . . This is Mom."

"Oh, hi, Mom."

"Hi, sweetie. I was thinking: For Sunday dinner, instead of doing it here, we can have it at your place. What do you think?"

My mom was a stickler for eating meals together. When I was with Jeff, she made attempts to come over when I couldn't make it home, but the traffic was too much. Once I moved back home, we tried to keep them up more regularly, at least twice a month.

"Uh, sure. That sounds good. Just us, or are you bringing Aunt Pam?"

"I'll check to see if she's free or if she's planning to go to her weekly bingo night. And no need to cook anything; I'll bring the food over."

"Okay; sounds good. Just let me know the time."

"Will do, sweetie. Talk to you soon. Love you!"

"Love you, too, Mom."

A little disappointed that it wasn't Ryan calling, I checked my phone for any messages. No texts or calls. I impulsively decided to text him to see how his day was going, partly because the silence was unusual. But also, I just missed him.

Kamryn: Hello, Mr. Ellis? How's the day treating you?

A few seconds later, my office phone rang again. I smiled. Definitely Ryan.

"Hello? Kamryn Hanover," I answered after one ring again.

"Hello, Kamryn. Long time, no speak."

I instantly froze at my desk, and the smile I wore faded. I felt goosebumps crawl over my arms and legs as the voice on the other end of the phone pierced through my head. *Jeff.*

"Who is this?" I asked, noticing the shakiness in my voice.

"Oh, don't tell me you don't remember the sound of my voice. Has it been that long?"

"How did you get this number?"

"Not too many Kamryn Hanovers in the city working for big advertising firms. And since you haven't been accepting my calls or texts, I had to do some digging."

Alpine Bloom's website. They posted pictures and bios of their marketing and design teams. As the assistant director, I was now listed on the site. A quick Google search and a call to the receptionist, and anyone could have my direct line.

"Jeff, what do you want?" I asked, trying to sound firm.

"Well, at first, I wanted to talk, but now, I don't know. How about an explanation?"

"An explanation? For what?"

"For why you left me without a word and you've refused to talk to me since then."

"I don't owe you anything. Your actions should have been all the explanation you needed, so figure it out yourself and leave me alone."

"That's not how this works, Kamryn. We shared a life together. You're my fiancé, for Christ's sake!"

"Was your fiancé! And you shared a life with me and everyone else, or did you forget?"

"I told you that none of those women mattered. You're still holding on to things from years ago. I'm nothing like that anymore."

"Oh, yeah? So, Jenny didn't matter, either? You slept with her behind my back for months, and somehow, she doesn't matter?" I talked closely into the receiver, trying to keep my voice down.

"I am not the father of her baby. Jenny was a mistake. We were both vulnerable, and we let our emotions get the best of us, Kam. That's it."

"That's it? She's pregnant, Jeff!"

"But not with my child! She has a husband and whoever else she's been sleeping with. She doesn't know if I'm the father for sure."

"It doesn't even matter, Jeff. You slept with your boss's wife and my friend. Whether you're the father of her child like she claims you are, I could care less."

"So, you're willing to throw away our future over one mistake?"

"One mistake? What about your assistant?"

I could hear Jeff sighing with exasperation and sucking his teeth.

"What about her? I told you, I never slept with her."

"So, she just happened to be cruising around with you for another reason, right?"

"I gave her a ride home. That doesn't mean I slept with her."

"You know, I spoke with her, and she lied about being in your car."

"What are you talking about? When did you speak with her?"

"After the accident. I called her, and she lied. Why would she lie if you were just giving her a ride home?"

"I don't know, Kamryn. Maybe you intimidated her. But all of that is over. There are no other women, Kamryn. Just you."

"I don't care. We're not together anymore, so you can have as many women as you want."

"I can fix this, Kamryn. I can make this all go away. Just talk to me so we can move past this. Can we meet for dinner?"

"Jeff, I'm not interested in dinner or anything else. So, please stop calling."

"Are you seeing someone else?"

"Excuse me?" I asked suspiciously.

"Pretty strange that you're so quick to cut me loose this time. There must be another reason."

"You're delusional. I don't need another reason other than the hundred reasons you gave me. Now, leave me alone."

"This isn't over, Kamryn. We just need more time to work . . ."

"It's over for me."

And with that, I hung up the phone. I didn't realize it during the call, but my heart was racing, and my ears were warm. The building was always cold enough to cool a summer block, but right now, I was on fire. Hearing his voice startled my world. He managed to creep back into my existence with one call. I took a few deep breaths as my phone rang again. I could ignore calls and texts on my cell phone, but I would have to call IT in the morning to have his number blocked.

"Hello?" I asked sharply.

"May I speak with Kamryn Hanover?"

"Who is this?"

"Ryan Ellis."

"Oh. Hey," I said as I took another deep breath. How could I not recognize his voice?

"Hey. Are you okay?" he asked, sounding very concerned.

"Yeah, sorry. Just a little shaken; that's all."

"Shaken? What's going on? I barely recognized you when you answered the phone."

"Nothing. I'm okay," I said, trying to steady my breathing.

"You sure?" Still concerned.

"Yeah, just a lot happening around the office. But everything is okay. How are you?" I said, quickly changing the subject.

"I'm okay. It's been a little hectic today, and I just saw your message, so I decided to call."

"Oh, okay." I tried my best to gather myself together, but it took me a while to steady my thoughts and breathing.

"Sounds like we're both having a rough day. How about dinner tonight?"

"That sounds nice. Do you have early meetings tomorrow?" I asked, feeling calmer at the thought of seeing him later.

"Why? Are you planning to keep me up late tonight?" I could hear him smile through the phone.

"Maybe. We'll just have to see how the night goes." I chuckled.

"You have me intrigued, Ms. Hanover."

"What time do you want to come over? I just have to stop and pick up some groceries."

"I have groceries if you want to cook at my place."

"That works, too. What time should I meet you there?"

"I might be a little late leaving here, so you can head straight to my place when you get off."

"Um, okay. How will I get in?"

"Security has a spare key. I'll ask them to give it to you."

"Oh. Okay, if that works for you."

"You sound so nervous . . . Everything okay?"

"Sure. Just don't know if you want me alone to snoop around your place. I might find something." I chuckled again.

"I have nothing to hide, so snoop away, beloved."

"Okay. So, I'll see you tonight."

"Looking forward to it."

Another night with Ryan to look forward to. I was utterly shocked that he was so willing to let me in his place when he wasn't home. I would have to whip up something special in the kitchen tonight. I checked the call log in my phone to see what number Jeff had called me from. I was going to have to screen calls at work, the same way I did on my cell phone. I opened an email to send to IT as a reminder to put in a request to have his number blocked.

Jeff was starting to cross the line. I was so upset on the call that I'd forgotten to even ask if he had been following me. I haven't seen a silver BMW since I was at my mom's house, so maybe I was just imagining things. Even if he knew where I worked, he didn't know where I lived. Maybe this call was what he needed to know that we were officially done. Jenny had stopped reaching out with her apologies, as well. The only one left was Mrs. Rose.

She had grown quite fond of me over the years. She always reached out to me when she couldn't reach her son, which was fairly often. And, of course, I always answered. Now, she was emailing to have lunch. I hadn't responded to her yet, still deciding on whether I wanted to deal with a Rose family member.

Lauren and I were finally getting back to normal, so I'm sure she provided the details to her mother that Jeff didn't. Either way, there was nothing to discuss.

My phone chimed with a message.

Ryan: You can park in the garage. Use the code to open the door: 1196.

Kamryn: Okay, thanks!

Ryan: Don't be late. ;-)

I smiled, looking down at his text as I typed my response.

Kamryn: I wouldn't dream of it. Hope you're not too tired. ;-)

Ryan: I'll always have energy for you, beloved.

CHAPTER 22
Dinner for Two

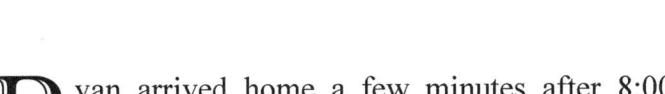

Ryan arrived home a few minutes after 8:00 p.m. to the aroma of spices and grilled steak coming from the kitchen. He walked through the door just as Kamryn was removing the lobster risotto from the stove. Somehow, she had managed to cook a surf and turf meal, his favorite, with ingredients that he was certain he didn't have in the fridge.

"Is that fresh lobster?" he asked as he approached the kitchen island.

"Yes, it is." She smiled.

"Where did that come from?"

"Same place as the steak and asparagus, the supermarket. I didn't like my options, so I went back out to the store."

"Ahhh, I see."

"Are you disappointed?" she asked him while biting her bottom lip.

"Disappointed that you went through great lengths to prepare my favorite meal? Not in the slightest." He walked around the island and stood directly in front of her.

252

"Favorite? I had no idea," she lied.

"I've never come home to a woman cooking in my kitchen besides my mom, so you have to tell me what's customary. Am I allowed to put my arms around you and kiss in the kitchen, or do you make me wash my hands first?"

"Hugs and kisses for me are always customary."

"Good."

Ryan was surprised by the overwhelming emotion he felt watching Kamryn navigate through the kitchen. It had been a long time since he had been in the presence of a woman in this element. The last time he allowed himself to fall in love, it blew up in his face. He never wanted to experience love that way again. Now, being around Kamryn stirred up those old feelings he thought were long buried. Although he knew Kamryn wasn't Simone, he wasn't ready to take that risk. Simone was a disaster, although it didn't initially start that way with her. She came into his life like a cool breeze and left like a hurricane, trying to take everything with her, including his sanity. Simone was beautiful, educated, and sophisticated, but she lacked morality, good judgment, and a kind heart. These were the qualities he was admiring more and more every day with Kamryn.

Simone was an excellent manipulator and conniving in all of her ways. He didn't understand how someone so talented could use and hurt people the way she did. She told him she loved him, and then tried to destroy him for loving her. Of course, Kamryn had been right. Simone was a model. She also ran several businesses, which is what first attracted him to her in the first place; that, and her looks. She was definitely beautiful. But none of that could make up for the amount of craziness she brought into his life. Since then, he learned to keep women at a distance from his personal life. He had a few entanglements here and there, but nothing past the bedroom.

He didn't realize peace existed in a relationship until he started dating Kamryn. Technically, they weren't even dating, as they had meticulously avoided being seen outside together since they started sleeping together. No dinner dates, no movie dates, not even a store run together. He threw in a suggestion here and there, but she always had a reason as to why she couldn't make it. Unless it was a group setting, then she had a reason to be around in the public eye. He respected her privacy, but also wondered if she just wasn't ready to be seen in public with someone other than Jeff. He had been her other half for years, and now, here he was, forcing her to move on. In fact, Ryan wasn't certain that she had moved on completely.

In the last few weeks, Jeff had called, texted, and emailed all throughout the night when he was around her. So, he was pretty sure he was reaching out during the day, too. He often wanted to ask her why she hadn't blocked his number, since he was clearly being a disturbance, but refrained every time the thought popped in his head. The last thing he wanted to do was make her uncomfortable or let her know that he had been uncomfortable seeing her phone go off at all hours in the middle of the night.

As they sat at the table eating her delicious meal, Ryan listened to her talk about her work projects. She was enjoying her time at Alpine Bloom. He was happy for her, although he suspected that her coworker, Daniel, liked her more than she let on. No need in pointing that out now and revealing that he was a tad bit jealous.

"So, how about you? You said work was pretty crazy today. What happened?" she asked.

"Nothing that won't resolve itself; just a misunderstanding with investors."

"Investors? That's interesting."

"Not really. It's all quite boring."

"Why are you so secretive about work?" she asked, with a pondering look that got his attention.

"I don't intend to be. I'd just rather hear about you and your day more so than mine."

"Hmm . . . I don't buy that, but if that's what you're selling, I'll back off."

She picked up her plate and wine glass and sashayed toward the kitchen.

"Dessert?"

"Dessert? You mean there's more?" Ryan asked, following behind her.

"There's always dessert after dinner."

"Well, I was kind of hoping that would be you," he responded and snuggled up behind her while placing his plate on the counter.

Kamryn turned to face him and kissed him enough to make him want to take her clothes off in the kitchen.

"This is only part two of your meal tonight. What you have coming later will definitely be a grand finale."

"Are we allowed to skip to the showstopper?" Ryan noticed his voice had grown huskier than usual. He wanted her badly.

"Nope. So, how about you go into the living room, put on the TV, and relax while I finish prepping? Can you do that for me?"

As Ryan looked into her face, he wanted to tell her that he would do anything for her. She could make him do anything without hesitation. In that moment, and every moment they shared together, she had him addicted. There was no way he could deny that he was falling for her. If I had the courage, I would tell her right here and now how I feel about her. I've wanted to be with her, always. Not just behind closed doors, sharing stories, and intimacy—but everywhere that the laws allow. I want her to be mine.

"Yes, I can do that." That's all he said as he planted a firm kiss on Kamryn's lips.

*****

Kamryn

Ryan was absolutely mesmerizing. I twirled around his kitchen, singing love songs in my head. I remembered they used to make me uncomfortable, people confessing their undying love and loyalty in their words while I was going through turmoil in my relationship. These days, the words had a sudden spark to them. They ignited a flame inside me that I thought burned out long ago. I'm sure I'm not in love with Ryan, but it feels good to hear a song and think of someone other than Jeff.

I pulled the cookie brownies out of the oven to prevent them from cooking through. Nobody likes a hard cookie or brownie. I poked a fork in one of them to test for an oozing chocolate center. *Perfect.* I learned early on that Ryan and I both shared a sweet tooth. While I was trying to starve my cravings, Ryan had every sugary dessert known to man in his home. I grabbed the ice cream from the fridge and scooped a healthy portion of French vanilla ice cream onto his dish. Once the fudge sauce was finished heating, I sprinkled a few swirls over his dessert and skipped mine. It's the least I could do for myself to save these hips from spreading to the next season.

As I walked into the living room, I noticed Ryan had changed his clothes and was flipping through the channels. He'd made my mouth water earlier when he came home in tailored slacks and a white button-up shirt with no tie. But now, even in his sweat shorts and T-shirt, he looked absolutely delectable, almost as good as this dessert.

"I see I'm going to have to put in an extra hour at the gym tomorrow," Ryan said, eyeing the dessert as I placed it in front of him.

"Oh, please. You can even afford to skip a day if you wanted to."

"Not if you keep this up. I'm still stuffed from dinner, which was amazing, by the way. Thank you."

"If it's too much, we can skip dessert." I playfully tried to remove his latte from the coffee table.

"Now, let's not be wasteful. I'm sure I can find room for this somewhere," he said, taking the plate back.

"How often do you work out, anyway?" I asked.

"At least five times a week, but usually, I do a little every day."

"Wow. That's impressive."

"It comes with the line of work."

"What do you mean?"

"The first business I purchased was a gym. I wasn't in the best shape, and I couldn't afford to pay a ton of models to promote the company. So, I started working out so I could pay myself and attract clients. After a while, it became a habit for me. It's hard to walk into your place of business and encourage people when you don't practice what you preach."

"Which gym do you own?" I asked, intriguinged.

I could tell he hesitated for a moment before answering my question.

"Bodied Fitness."

"Sweet! Mica and I were going to sign up there a while back. Which one do you own?"

Another short pause from Ryan. He took another lick of the spoon before responding.

"All of them."

"Like, the entire franchise?" I squeaked, trying to swallow my own ice cream.

"Yeah. It's just a few of them."

"A few? There are at least twenty!"

"Eleven," he corrected me.

"Wow. That's really amazing! Who knew? I bet your family is proud."

"Yeah, they are. They still think I run the one gym I opened up years ago."

"Why haven't you told them about the others?"

"I don't know. My mom is a proud mama, so she loves to brag about me and my siblings. It can be a little uncomfortable, so I found it best to keep some things to myself."

"Ah, I see. Well, I feel like I should be telling you congratulations or something. You've accomplished so much. and you're only in your thirties."

"I had a couple of good investments early on. My dad helped me with that. He made sure I invested every dime I earned, and he taught me young. So, by the time I graduated college, he supported my idea of investing in small businesses."

"Businesses? You have others besides Bodied Fitness?"

"Just a few others, but Bodied Fitness is my baby. The old owner decided to sell and relocate once the business took off, and I offered to buy his shares. I put all my focus into it, so it's really the core of everything we do. Everything else just kind of took off from there."

"Wow. This is really amazing. I honestly had no idea. No wonder your place is so nice." I chuckled and looked around his living room, actually taking it all in.

Ryan lived in a gated community in what I later discovered was an upper class area. The security officers only let in cars with recognized plates or coded access. The homes in the community were immaculate, but Ryan's was a little smaller. He still had a ton of space and at least two bedrooms I hadn't even seen yet. I always figured he inherited the place from his parents once they decided to move out of the city.

"Thank you," he responded.

"Does this make you uncomfortable?"

"What does?"

"Sharing this information. I can tell you don't do it often, so I'm surprised you're willing to tell me. But I get the sense that it makes you uneasy."

"It does. I had a few unpleasant experiences in the past, so I take more precautions now. But not with you." He looked at me intensely.

"Well, that's good to know. And I won't sell your secrets to the National Enquirer, if that's what you're worried about." I offered my friendliest smile.

"Good to know, but I trust you."

"Oh! I almost forgot the dessert wine! Give me your glass," I said as I hopped off the couch and scurried into the kitchen.

"No more food, baby. I'm stuffed," he yelled, and I heard him flipping through the channels again.

"It's just a little wine!" I yelled from the kitchen.

I finally found the wine opener after rustling through several drawers. I poured two glasses and headed back into the living with my final surprise of the night. Then, suddenly, I stopped dead in my tracks as I heard the newscaster on the television. I was frozen solid, and I couldn't breathe. Both glasses slipped through my hands and shattered to the floor. I saw Ryan get up from the couch and come towards me. His lips were moving, but I couldn't hear any of the words from his mouth. The room was silent, spinning, and moving in slow motion. The only thing I heard was the headline on the TV as a picture of Jenny flashed across the screen.

"Jennifer Lancaster, a thirty-four-year-old woman, went missing in the East Charleston area last week. She was last seen leaving a local shopping mall that she is known to frequent. Lancaster is married to the CEO of Global Investments, David

Lancaster. Mr. Lancaster reported his wife missing after being unable to reach her for a few days. Upon returning home from a business trip, he contacted the police when it became evident that Mrs. Lancaster had not been in the home for a few days. Lancaster had reportedly told a family member that she was meeting an acquaintance for dinner the last time they spoke but did not provide the details. It is not known what she was wearing at the time of her disappearance, but police have released the video footage of her leaving the shopping mall earlier that day. Mrs. Lancaster is reported to be five feet, six inches tall and 145 pounds, and was last seen leaving the Charleston Shopping Center at around 4 p.m. Mr. Lancaster, who was unreachable for comments, has told police that he is concerned for his wife's safety and is praying for her safe return home. If anyone has information, please contact the Charleston Police Department at the number on the screen."

"Baby, are you okay? Kamryn, Kamryn . . . Talk to me. What's wrong?"

I slowly heard Ryan's voice echoing in my head, bringing me back to reality. He was standing in front of me holding my arms, trying to guide me toward the couch to have a seat. Once I was seated, I heard him walk over to his iRobot vacuum to clean up the glass I'd shattered on the floor. He kneeled in front of me, and I finally made eye contact with him.

"Kamryn. Baby, please talk to me. What's going on?"

"It's Jenny."

"Who?" he asked, sounding confused.

"Jenny, my friend, the one who was sleeping with Jeff. They just showed her picture on the news. She's missing."

CHAPTER 23
Where's Jenny?

The next morning, I called Mica on my way to work to tell her what I saw on the news last night.

"Kamryn! I've been trying to reach you all night! Where have you been?" she asked as soon as she answered the phone.

Realizing that I still hadn't told my friend that I was sleeping with her boyfriend's best friend, I decided to lie.

"I stayed over at my mom's place. My phone must have died, and I didn't have it on the charger," I responded with a partial truth.

"Did you see the news?" she asked.

"Yes; that's why I'm calling. I'm freaking out, Mica!"

"Why are you freaking out?"

"Because Jeff called me yesterday."

"And you answered?" she questioned.

"He called my job phone. And before you ask, he must have done a Google search of my name, and it popped up on Alpine Bloom's website."

"And what did he do, call the operator until he was transferred to you?"

"I guess so."

"So, what did he say?"

"The same thing he always says: We need to talk; they're lying; it wasn't me. Basic Jeff nonsense."

"That man doesn't stray far from his playbook, I see." I could hear Mica rolling her eyes through the phone.

"But he knows I know about Jenny. I confronted him about it, and he said it's not his child."

Mica didn't respond but scoffed loudly through the phone.

"What if he did something?" I asked.

"What do you mean?"

"Well, he asked me what if he could make it go away, and I told him I didn't care. I mean, I thought he was talking about asking her for an abortion, but now, I don't know. What if?"

"Do you think he's capable of doing something crazy like kidnapping a whole human—who happens to also be his boss's wife?"

"I don't know, Mica! That's why I'm asking you."

"Well, didn't you say that Jenny wanted to leave town?"

"Yeah. So?"

"Well, maybe she pulled one of your moves and packed up her stuff and got out of town."

"Yeah, maybe." I pondered the thought, attempting to calm my nerves.

"Plus, she was planning to leave her husband. She said that herself. So, I really wouldn't be surprised if she left while he was away so she wouldn't have to explain her predicament."

"Yeah, that's true, too. I would think that's the last thing she wanted was public embarrassment."

"Heck, I don't blame her."

"But what about what Lauren said to me?"

"What did she say?"

"I told you. At your game night, she basically told me to stay away from Jeff because he's dangerous."

"Yeah. So?" Mica asked.

"Well, isn't that suspicious?"

"Coming from his sister who happens to hate his guts as much as I do, no. And Jeff is dangerous. Dangerously conceited, obnoxious, and reckless."

"So, you don't think I should go to the police?"

"The police?"

"Yeah, to tell them what I know about her being pregnant by Jeff."

"Do we know for sure it's Jeff's baby?"

"No, but I know they were having an affair."

"So, maybe that's something to tell David, and then he can tell the police."

"Oh, gosh, Mica. You want me to tell the woman's husband that she was having an affair? He's probably worried to death, and I'm just supposed to call him up and tell him this?"

"Kamryn, if you're feeling compelled to say something, it's him or the police. So, what do you want to do?"

"Neither."

"And that's okay, too, but I know you'll change your mind."

We chatted for a few more minutes in incredulity at the possibility that Jenny could actually be missing or on a runaway train somewhere. I pulled into the parking lot at my job and sat in silence for a few minutes. I scrolled through my phone several times, thinking of someone to call to debate my next move, but no one came to mind. Surprisingly, I didn't have David's number, so I would have to call the office in order to reach him. But who do I call? The only numbers I had were Jeff's direct line and the number to his assistant. I needed to think of another game plan.

My phone rang and startled me so much that I dropped it on the floor of the car, causing me to struggle a little to retrieve it.

"Hello?"

"Hey. Just checking in? How are you feeling?" Ryan asked.

"I'm doing okay."

"You don't sound okay. Is there anything I can do?"

"Not really, but thanks for asking."

"Tell me what you're thinking about."

I hadn't told Ryan about Jeff's call, and I didn't want to give him a reason to feel concerned, so I kept it to myself for now.

"I feel like I just saw her. One moment, she's standing in front of me, telling me she's sleeping with Jeff; then, the next, her face is plastered all over the evening news as a missing person."

"Yeah, it's unsettling. I can't imagine how that feels."

"I mean, she was my friend for years. We hung out together, shopped together, and shared stories and drinks through the good and the bad. Even if I never planned on speaking to her again, it's just scary to think that she's in danger."

"I can't believe it myself. Do you know anyone in her family?"

"Not personally. I know of them, but we only hung out together or with the guys at work functions."

"Go it. So, no one you can call to check in with."

"Yeah, not really."

"Where are you now? Still driving to work?"

"No. I'm here, sitting in the parking lot."

"Are you sure you want to go in today?"

"I don't want to call out. I'm still kind of new, and we have a ton of projects going on."

"Have you had breakfast?"

"No."

"You promised me you would get something to eat on the way."

"I was a little distracted." Talking to Mica caused me to drive past several drive-throughs that I could have picked up breakfast from.

"How about I pick you up from work today, so you don't have to drive home? I don't want you to be alone."

"No, that's too much. I'll be okay, I promise."

"You already broke one promise today. You sure you want to aim for another so soon?"

I contemplated Ryan's offer for a moment. It would be nice to have his company.

"I may not be good company, Ryan. I don't want to ruin your mood."

"That's not possible. And I know you're upset, and you have a lot on your mind. I just want to try and ease the burden of your thoughts for a little while. Okay?"

"I appreciate it." God, this man is perfect in more ways than I can count.

I brushed through the day as fast as I could just to get to 5:00 p.m. I attended meetings, took calls, spoke to clients, and still couldn't recall a single event of the day. Ryan promised to be here by five, even though I told him I would wait around until he got off. By 5:02 p.m., he was texting me to let me know he was downstairs in the lobby. I didn't hesitate. I grabbed my purse, cell phone, and laptop and was in the elevator before I could blink. As the doors were closing, someone stuck their hand in, causing the door to reopen.

"Hey. You're headed home early today," Daniel said as he stepped onto the elevator.

"Yeah. Not early, just on time. How about you?"

"Yeah, I should be out of here by 5:30 p.m. I just have to go over a few proposals and send them to Margaret."

"Anything I can help with?"

"Sure. Maybe I'll email them to you, too, and you can let me know your thoughts."

"Okay. I'll check when I get home." The elevator reached the lobby, and I hurried off to meet Ryan. "Night, Daniel. Talk to you tomorrow."

"It's cool. I'll walk you to your car."

"Oh. Well, my ride is already here," I said awkwardly.

Ryan looked up from his phone as he heard my heels coming across the lobby floor. He smiled and walked towards me to greet me. I noticed that Daniel was still trailing behind me, unaware that I was walking toward the sexy man in the lobby.

"Hey. You all set?"

"Yeah, I'm ready." I turned around to see if Daniel had finally realized that I didn't need assistance today, but he was still standing there with a clumsy look on his face.

"Ryan, this is my coworker . . ."

"Daniel, right?" Ryan interjected and extended his hand toward Daniel.

"Yeah." Daniel slowly returned the offer and shook Ryan's hand, obviously confused.

"Nice to meet you. Ryan Ellis. Kamryn's told me a lot about the work that you both do. Always very interesting," Ryan continued while firmly placing his hand across my lower back and leaning me towards him.

"Uhhh . . . thanks. Nice to meet you," Daniel responded, still unaware that Ryan was clearly trying to outshine him in this pissing contest.

"I'll see you tomorrow, Daniel. Don't forget to email me if you need my help with anything."

"Will do. See you tomorrow." And with that, Daniel turned and headed back towards the elevators.

"Are you done?" I asked, turning back to Ryan.

"Huh?"

"Was it really necessary to show all of your testosterone?"

"What do you mean?" he asked, pretending to not know what I'm referring to.

"Ugh. Let's just go."

I sat in silence for most of the ride home. I had absolutely no energy to argue with Ryan while still being concerned about Jenny and weary about Jeff.

"I'm sorry, Kamryn."

"What?" I asked, looking over at him as he drove.

"I'm sorry. I didn't mean to act that way or embarrass you in front of your coworker. I know how unprofessional that is. I really am sorry."

"Why did you do that?" I asked, still unmoved by his apology at the moment.

"I honestly don't know. I don't have an excuse."

"You know why you did it, so just tell me."

He took a second to think about what he wanted to tell me before responding to my questions.

"And please don't lie," I urged.

"I know he likes you. Seeing him walking behind you made me a little jealous."

"A little?"

"Okay, more than a little." Ryan looked over at me and grabbed my hand from my lap.

"So, what if he likes me? He's my coworker, and last time I checked, I was sleeping with you. So, what's the issue?"

"There is no issue, love."

"Are you sure?"

Ryan slowed the car down and pulled over into a gas station. I peered over at the dashboard to check if the tank was low, but it was full. He put the car in park and turned in his seat to face me.

"What are you doing?" I asked.

"I want to focus on this conversation. Are you upset with me?"

"Yes, a little," I answered honestly.

"I'll do anything to fix that. I really am sorry about how I acted. I can tell from the way you talk about him that he likes you. A lot. And part of me wanted him to know that you were taken, even if it's only sexually. I am and was a little jealous, but again, that's no reason to behave like that and make the man uncomfortable."

"Do you think I like him? Is that it?"

"I don't know. It doesn't matter. I should have kept my cool."

"And you pulled over to tell me that?"

"I can tell that you're upset, and I don't want it to linger."

"Okay. It's fine."

He grabbed my hand again and pulled it toward him, kissing the back.

"Am I forgiven?"

"I didn't think you'd be asking that question so soon," I responded.

"Neither did I. I'm a little ashamed of what just happened."

"Let's just go home."

CHAPTER 24
What day is it?

R yan stayed over at my house for the next three nights to keep me company. This gave us plenty of time to make up after the stunt he pulled in the lobby with Daniel. I was a little annoyed, but I forgave him as soon as we walked through the door. Heck, I've forgiven worse. I'd never seen Ryan so unsure of himself, with eyes like a puppy dog's, sulking with his head in his hands. It's not as if he didn't apologize five times on the car ride to my place, but he was just as distraught once we made it upstairs.

I rolled over in my bed, trying not to disturb him, and checked the news alerts on my phone. No updates about Jenny's whereabouts, and she was still missing. Jeff was still texting and calling me as if he didn't see that his mistress was headlining the news. Ironically, it gave me a little comfort that he was still doing his normal outreach. He couldn't possibly have kidnapped a woman and still be reaching out to me to make up. I still hadn't found a way to contact the office and speak with David without Jeff or his assistant finding out, nor had I contacted the police. For now, all I could do was wait and hope that Jenny had found her way across the world and was safely preparing for the arrival of her child.

"Are you up?"

I heard Ryan's groggy voice behind me, locked my phone, and faced him.

"Hey. I see you're finally up," I said as I snuggled up close to him.

"Any news?" he asked.

"About what?"

"Your friend. The one that's missing."

I looked at him in silence, curious as to how he knew that I was searching for updates about Jenny.

"You check every morning, Kamryn. I know you're still worried about it," he asked after I didn't respond.

"Sorry."

"Don't be. I just wish there was something that I could do to help clear your head."

"I can think of a few things," I say as I reach for his body parts under the covers.

"I'm beginning to think that you're using sex as a distraction." Ryan glanced over at me and let out a low moan.

"Welp, you offered to help me and be here in my time of need." I grinned.

"It's the Lord's day, and you're starting up already, huh?" he joked.

"We've already sinned today, Moses. It's nearly 2:00 in the afternoon."

"And whose fault is that? We were up until 6:00 in the morning," he said, now leaning over me.

"A little bit of both." I smiled up at him.

"I must admit, you are irresistible. But after this, I need nourishment." Ryan nestled his head into my warmth as my eyes gently closed.

After our afternoon love session, Ryan decided to go for a run in the gym in the building to stretch his muscles. Funny, I lived here for almost a month and hadn't stepped foot in that place yet. I prefer to jog in the fresh air outside. While he was gone, I whipped up some food for a quick brunch to offer him the nourishment he so deeply craved. I heard the key through the door and started to move a little faster in the kitchen.

"Well, hello there."

I turned to see Ryan's glistening body in gym trunks and tank top that was drenched with enough sweat to fill a pool.

"Hello yourself, sexy," I said, evidently giving him a seductive look.

"Keep it up. You're going to wear him out," he said as he planted a kiss on my lips.

"I won't bother you now. Maybe after we eat." I gave him a wink.

We lay around for most of the day, watching TV and occasionally switching to the news. Ryan had grown accustomed to my patterns and didn't hassle me about it. Instead, he just held my hand and offered comfort throughout the day.

"What are your plans for the rest of the day?"

"I don't know, maybe do some cleaning."

"How about we go to the movies? Get out of the house and get some fresh air."

I gave it a quick thought and realized that we had each been cooped up indoors for a few days, besides leaving the house to go to work. In fact, we hadn't been out together alone since we went to the Blue Lagoon.

"That actually sounds like a great idea."

"Really?" Ryan turned to me on the couch and gave me a surprised look.

"Yeah. Let me go shower and start getting ready," I said, standing up from the sofa.

"Oh. Well, in that case, I'll come join you." Ryan chased after me.

I got out of the shower to the sound of my intercom ringing. Ryan stepped out and grabbed a towel, also curious as to who could be ringing the bell.

"Expecting guests today?" he asked as he dried the water from his head.

"Not that I know of." I quickly dried off my damp body and wrapped my robe around my body to check the camera.

"Oh, my God! Ryan!" I shrieked, standing by the foyer.

Ryan came running out of the bedroom with the towel wrapped around his waist.

"What is it? Who's at the door?"

"It's my mother! It's Sunday!"

"Yeah, I know it's Sunday. Did you know she was coming over?" he asked, trying to squeeze his towel even tighter over his waist.

"Yes. We're supposed to be having Sunday dinner, but I forgot."

I glanced back at the video intercom as they were entering the building. A neighbor was exiting and now holding the door for them.

"Oh, my God. They're coming up! Get dressed!"

"They?!" For the first time, I heard him panic.

"My mom and my aunt! Oh, my God! I have to find something to wear! I should have cleaned the house. OMG! Where's the Febreze?!"

"Febreze? What do you need Febreze for?" I could see Ryan struggling to put his boxers on.

"We've been going at it for three days! The house smells like sex!"

"Kamryn, calm down for a second, baby. Just breathe." He took hold of my shoulders and stood in front of me. "The house smells like Air Wick plug-ins, not sex. Now, just calm down so we can do one thing at a time. What do you want me to do?"

At that moment, the doorbell rang. I looked down at my silk robe, clinging to my naked body, and at Ryan, standing in his fitted boxers with one arm through his undershirt.

"Get dressed. I'll get the door."

I tightened my robe and headed towards the door, taking a deep breath before swinging the door open to greet my family.

"Mom! Aunt Pam! How are you?"

"Hi, sweetie! How are you? Why are you so out of breath?" my mom asked as she kissed my cheek and breezed past me to the kitchen, pulling her mini utility cart with food trays and pans.

"My little Kammy! Just as beautiful as ever. How are you, deary?"

"I'm good, Aunt Pam. How are you doing?" She, too, kissed my cheek and headed behind my mother to the kitchen.

"I got my health, so I'm doing great," she said from the kitchen.

"I thought we were having dinner at 6:00 p.m. today. What happened?" I tried to speak as calmly as possible.

"Well, if you checked your messages, you would know that I need to replace the oven light in my stove. Repair company can't come until tomorrow, so I need to cook the food here. Everything is prepped; just needs to go in the oven."

"Mom, you texted me? When?" I asked.

"I don't know, dear. Sometime this morning. What have you been up to today? You look flustered."

"Kammy, I love what you've done with the place! Your mom showed me pictures, but it looks absolutely marvelous in person." My Aunt Pam was now in the living room, admiring the space.

I was grateful for the interruption because I didn't have an answer ready for why I was so flustered and out of breath. Ryan was down the hall getting dressed in my bedroom. If I was lucky, he would sneak out of the window and shimmy down the wall like Spider-Man to save ourselves from embarrassment.

"Thank you, Auntie."

"Sweetie, how do you turn on this oven? These new appliances are absolutely dreadful for me to use."

I assisted my mother quickly in the kitchen, and then headed into the living room to see if I could distract my aunt while Ryan snuck out the front door. Suddenly, I heard a noise from the bedroom. My aunt obviously heard it, too, because she immediately turned in my direction.

"What was that?" she asked.

"What?" I pretended as if I'd heard nothing at all.

But then, as if on cue, the bedroom door opened, and I heard Ryan's bare footsteps slowly coming down the hall. I squeezed my eyes shut and imagined clicking my heels together, saying, "I wish I was home. I wish I was home." But I was home, and there was no escaping my present company and situation. I sensed Ryan's presence behind me and opened my eyes. My aunt was now smiling in my direction, but not at me. At Ryan.

"That," she responded.

"What's what?" my mom said, now coming out of the kitchen to see what all the fuss was about.

I didn't turn to look at Ryan, but I could feel him smiling at all the eyes on him from behind me.

"Hello," was all he said in a nervous voice.

"Angela, I think we know why she was out of breath when she opened the door." My aunt gave me a wink, then continued to smile at Ryan.

"Indeed, Pam. Indeed, we might."

✶✶✶✶✶

Ryan

I felt like exhibit A in a museum as I looked at the puzzled faces of Kamryn's mom and aunt, unsure of who was who. They were, in fact, identical, which is something Kamryn hadn't mentioned in our conversations about family characteristics. The room remained silent for a moment while everyone's eyes darted back and forth between Kamryn and me. I felt the heat rising from my shirt and looked down at Kamryn, who was experiencing her own discomfort. My natural instinct was to reach for her and wrap my arms around her, but I was equally as nervous and

"Yes. Michelle is dating Charlie, who is also a close friend of mine," I repeated myself due to extreme nervousness. I could feel the inquisition coming on.

"Well, isn't that nice. Best friends who are coupled with best friends." Aunt Pam smiled at her sister. The two shared a look that let me know they were speaking in their own language.

"Uhhh, yeah. Kinda," I responded, looking down at my feet.

"Kinda? You and Kammy are dating, aren't you?" she continued.

I paused, unsure of how to respond to our situation. I looked up from my feet, hoping that she was on her way back into the living room.

"Please don't tell me you're doing that friend with benefits thing, deary," her mom chimed in when I didn't respond in time.

"Um, no," I lied. "We're friends," I answered anxiously.

"So, you're not dating?" Aunt Pam followed up.

"We're getting to know each other," I said hesitantly.

"Mom." Kamryn walked into the living room, fully dressed.

"Yes? Glad you could join us, sweetie," her mom responded without taking her eyes off of me.

"Did I just hear you ask him if we're friends with benefits?" Kamryn asked, obviously stressed by the situation.

"Well, are you?" her mom asked again, looking at me and back at Kamryn.

"Mom! Please stop."

"Relax, sweetie. It's a simple question."

"We're just trying to learn more about your friend here, deary," Aunt Pam chimed in.

Kamryn and I shared a glance, and I got a sense that my presence was now making her uncomfortable.

"Maybe I should get going," I said as I rose from the couch. "It really was a pleasure to meet you both."

"Wait. You're not staying for dinner?" her mom asked.

"Please don't let us scare you off, Ryan. I promise we're harmless," Aunt Pam followed up.

Keeping up with the two of them was similar to going through a maze. Now matter which way you turned, you were trapped.

"I'm sorry, Ryan," Kamryn said softly, pleading with her eyes.

"Don't be," I responded and instinctively gave her a reassuring wink.

"So, you're staying for dinner?" her mom asked again.

I paused again, looking to Kamryn for assistance. I didn't want to abandon her, but I also knew how intrusive it could be to have a significant other around family when you weren't prepared to answer questions. And I wasn't her significant other. We were, in fact, friends with benefits, but I wouldn't admit to that. It's not a title I wanted with her. When Kamryn didn't answer the question, in my eyes, I made another attempt to politely escape.

"No, I should probably get going. I don't want to intrude."

"Oh, you're not intruding. Right, Kam?" her mom questioned.

"Looks like we may have intruded on you," Aunt Pam commented, winking at Kamryn.

"Kamryn?" her mother asked again, more firmly this time.

"You're not intruding, Ryan. You should stay," Kamryn finally responded.

"See? There. It's all settled!" her mom exclaimed with excitement and hurried back towards the kitchen.

I studied Kamryn's face, unsure if her decision to have me stay was completely her own or from her mother's influence . . . The look in her eyes showed desperation. But I was unsure if she was desperate for me to leave or have me stay. We looked at each other in silence for a moment, unable to read the cues we were sending each other.

"Are you sure?" I asked as I unconsciously reached for her hand, completely unaware that her mother had walked back into the room with champagne glasses. I was so focused on Kamryn that I forgot her aunt was still in the room, witnessing our non-verbal exchanges.

"Yes. Please stay," she said, not letting my hand go and giving it a soft squeeze.

"Oh, I like him, Angela," her aunt said with a grin as wide as the Pacific Ocean.

"Indeed, Pamela. I think I do, too. Let's do a toast before dinner." She extended her hands towards us so we could each take a glass, then scurried off again to the kitchen.

She returned with her own glass and a bottle of champagne.

"Here. Let me help you with that," I said, quickly taking the bottle from her to open it without spilling it on the floor.

As I poured the champagne, I got a sense that I was being observed. I glanced up, and, as expected, all eyes were on me. I placed the empty bottle on the coffee table and held my own glass.

"So, what shall we toast to, ladies? New friendships?" I asked, immediately embarrassed by my own question.

I looked at Kamryn, and she was smiling . . . almost laughing at me for making a fool of myself.

"Well, I don't know how new this is, but I like it," Aunt Pam said, clinking her glass to mine and then Kamryn's.

"Then, to new beginnings," her mom chimed in, raising her glass.

"Anything you'd like to add to that, Kammy?" she questioned her.

"I like new beginnings," she responded without taking her eyes off of me.

CHAPTER 25
Sunday Dinner
————⟡————

Sunday dinner went smoother than expected. Ryan was his usual charming self once his nerves settled. It was cute to see him so off balance around my mom and aunt. They were a tricky duo to handle, but he managed with ease. Of course, they questioned him about every detail of his life: what he did for a living, where he worked, his family history, and his future plans for his own family. I interjected at every opportunity but was quickly silenced by my mother. Every chance I had, I tried to remind them that he and I were just friends, so there was no need to question him this much. But Ryan simply gave me a small gesture each time to assure me that he was okay—a pat on my leg, a squeeze of my hand, or a subtle wink and smirk.

Somehow, sitting beside him at the table in front of my family felt natural. Watching him speak and steal glances at me throughout the night exposed me to a completely different side of him. His glances weren't sexual but instead reassuring, as if he was checking in on me through different moments of the evening. At one point, Ryan referred to us as "we" when discussing a movie that we both liked, and I could see my mom and aunt share a twin look. Ryan was referring to us as a couple, even though his mouth said "friends."

I could tell they were completely smitten by him, as well, with their relentless questions. I was grateful that Ryan had stayed. He had a way of easing the tension with his presence without ever moving a muscle.

"Well, I'm glad Kam has a friend like you, Ryan. Because after that last knucklehead, I almost wanted her to stay single," my mom stated.

"Are we still using the term 'friend' here? I thought we moved past that. You two are definitely more than friends," Aunt Pam chimed in as Ryan let out a soft chuckle.

"Aunt Pam, I told you. We *are* friends. There's no need to rush that into something else."

"Hmph. I don't see the point in waiting when you have a catch like that."

Ryan choked on his water as he sipped from his glass.

"No need to be modest, son. I think we can all see that you're a good catch, and you seem to care about Kammy," Aunt Pam continued.

"Yes, I do. She's a great catch for me, too," Ryan said, looking in my direction as I avoided eye contact.

"And like my sister said, you're a hell of a lot better than that last one." Aunt Pam shuddered as if she had a chill running through her body.

"That reminds me Kamryn, have you heard anything about your friend?" my mom asked.

"No; nothing yet."

"That's just so awful to think something could have happened to her. Just remember to block him so you don't have to talk to him anymore. You don't want another surprise call at work," my mother said as she got up to remove her plate from the table.

I cringed at my mother's comment because I hadn't mentioned it to Ryan. Hoping that he somehow didn't hear it, I opened my mouth to change the subject, but I was interrupted by my aunt.

"Yeah, your mom told me about that. As if calling your phone everyday isn't enough, he Googled you and managed to get your job line, too. Just shameful."

"It's okay, Auntie. I contacted IT to block him."

"Good. Your mom told me you were startled. I just couldn't imagine . . ." My aunt's voice trailed off as she, too, headed into the kitchen with her plate.

"Surprise call?" Ryan asked, looking at me.

"It's nothing."

"Nothing that you couldn't tell me," he asked again, showing more concern.

"I didn't want you to worry."

"Worry about what, exactly?"

I sighed, knowing that I couldn't escape the conversation that was about to ensue.

"Jeff called me at work this week. It was the first time we spoke in a while, so I was just a little startled to hear from him. That's all."

I heard the twins in the kitchen cleaning up the dishes and packing up the leftovers.

"When did this happen?"

"Wednesday. The same day I learned that Jenny was missing on the news."

"So, what did he say?"

"The same thing he always says. Lies and begging me to talk."

"Are you two finished? We're cleaning up. Let me get those plates," my mom said, walking over to us.

"It's okay, Mom. I'll get it."

"No; give them here, and we'll be out of your hair in just a few." She took the plates and headed back into the kitchen.

I looked over at Ryan, who was looking anywhere else in the room but at me.

"I promise it was nothing, Ryan. I didn't think . . ."

"Why didn't you tell me?" he asked as he gave me a look that pierced my soul.

"I just didn't think it was necessary."

"You didn't think it was necessary?" he asked in a tone that I had never heard from him.

"No. I didn't want to worry you, Ryan."

Just then, my mom and aunt came from the kitchen to say their goodbyes. I almost asked them to stay longer to avoid having the argument that was coming. They moved so quickly to collect their things that I barely had time to speak. I knew the twins were trying to leave so Ryan and I could enjoy the rest of the evening, but they had no idea the mess they had started right before their departure.

Ryan stood up from the table to, I thought, say goodbye to them, but instead walked towards the door to grab his shoes.

"I can walk you downstairs, ladies. I'm heading out myself."

"Oh, you don't have to leave on our account, Ryan. We know what you kids are up to." Aunt Pam gave him a wink.

"Yeah, we can manage. You two go enjoy the rest of your evening."

"I have an early morning, so I need to get some re—"

"Ryan, can you stay for a second? I need you to help me with something," I asked in a plea to get him to stay.

I didn't want to say in front of everyone that I wanted to talk and that he should stay. I walked over to meet him in the foyer and grabbed his hand, now a known gesture between the two of us. He looked down at me hesitantly, as if he knew exactly what I was up to. He looked over to the twins, who were anxiously awaiting his decision, before looking back to me.

"Sure," he said calmly.

I could tell that he was anything but calm. He was pissed and possibly hurt.

"Goodnight, you two!" The twins ushered out of the door.

"Text me when you both get home," I urged and locked the door.

I turned immediately to find Ryan standing in the middle of the living room with his arms folded, looking at me.

"Ryan . . ." I started to explain myself.

"What do you need help with?" He was being short with me.

"Nothing. I wanted you to stay," I answered honestly.

"I see lying is becoming a pattern for you."

"Ryan, I didn't lie to you. I just . . ."

"You mean the day I called you and you seemed flustered at work, and I asked you what was wrong repeatedly, and you told me it was nothing when he was the obvious reason? Or how about omitting pieces of your day when we talk just to avoid telling me that you still talk to your ex? Which one isn't a lie, Kamryn?"

He was calm—too calm. I could see there was a storm brewing inside, but spoke he so calmly, as if to avoid his own anger from erupting. I had nothing to offer him but an apology. I should have told him. He had been there when I found out about Jenny twice. I should have told him what triggered my fears that night I was at his place.

I walked over to him and stood directly in front of his chest. He didn't unfold his arms and just looked down at me. I placed both hands on his arms and gently pushed them down to his sides. I didn't know what to say to ease this tension, but I was willing to try.

"I'm sorry I kept this from you, and I'm sorry I lied. Regardless of my reasons, I should have been honest and told you what was going on."

"What happened to being honest with each other?" he asked softly.

"I have been honest with you about everything else. And I promise I will never keep anything from you ever again."

"What were your reasons?"

I looked down, embarrassed to answer the question. Finally touching me, he placed a hand on my chin to lift my head up to face him.

"Tell me."

"I didn't want to be a problem."

"A problem?" he asked in confusion.

"I didn't want you to think that I was a problem for you, bringing drama into your life with a crazy ex. I just wanted to protect our peace."

"Did you think I couldn't handle it?"

"I didn't want you to have to handle it. I can barely handle it."

Ryan wrapped both arms around my shoulders and pulled me in close. I leaned my head on his and tried my best to hold back the emotions from this week.

"Thank you for trying to protect us and me. But I would rather know what's going on so I can stand with you. You don't have to fight every battle by yourself, love."

I was too emotional to respond. I wrapped my arms around his waist and squeezed as tightly as I could. I want this. I need this comfort. But I don't deserve it.

"Is there anything else you need to tell me?"

"No."

"Okay. Let's go to bed."

Tonight, going to bed meant exactly that. It wasn't a key word for a night of passionate lovemaking. Instead, Ryan held me in his arms and caressed my back as we lay there. We lay in silence all night, watching reruns of old sitcoms. I wanted desperately to tell him that I loved him but opted to just lay there, snuggled quietly on his chest.

"Are you still upset with me?"

"No."

"I really am sorry," I said, moving my head to face him.

"All is forgiven, love," he said as he leaned his head to kiss me.

CHAPTER 26
Secret Rose

Finally agreeing to meet up with Mrs. Rose wasn't an easy decision. She pretty much called and texted me weekly, asking me if we could talk and have lunch. She probably just wanted to check on her son. Jeff's relationship with his mother had been strained over the years. They talked very little. In fact, when she called the house, she mostly chatted with me for a few minutes before rushing off to attend one of her events or meetings. Always the socialite, Mrs. Rose kept herself busy with her magazine company and her frequent photo shoots.

We agreed to meet for dinner before I headed over to Mica's place for another game night. Thank goodness it was Friday. I could finish work, tell Mrs. Rose to stop contacting me because I was done with her son, and have a drink with friends while I stared at Ryan from across the room. Ryan. That had become our thing now, texting and stealing glances while we were in mixed company. The sneakiness and excitement usually left me hot and bothered and ready to take him home by the end of the night. As I smiled off into a daze, my phone chimed. Ryan. I swear this man has an extrasensory perception because he always texts or calls me when I have him on my mind, which has been very often lately.

Ryan: Hey, beautiful. How's work?

Kamryn: Hey . . . Work is okay. How's your day going?

Ryan: Busy, but it's getting better now.

Kamryn: Glad to hear it's improving. What time are you heading to Michelle's place tonight?

Ryan: Around the same time that you get there. ☺

Kamryn: I'll be a little late tonight . . . I have dinner plans first. Hoping it'll be quick.

Ryan: Dinner? Like a dinner date?

Kamryn: No, more like closing a chapter.

Ryan: Hmm . . . Sounds interesting.

Kamryn: Well, you know I live a very interesting life. ;-)

My phone chimed again, this time with a FaceTime call coming in from Ryan.

"Hey . . . You missed my face?" I asked playfully.

"I always do."

Ryan responded with a smile and a tone that was starting to become so soothing and dangerous at the same time.

"So, how long do I have to wait for you to grace me with your presence tonight?"

"I shouldn't be long. I've been putting this off for a while, so I'm hoping it'll be quick and painless." I chuckled.

Ryan stopped sorting through papers on his desk and looked at me more seriously on the phone. He paused for a few seconds, which instantly made my stomach do nervous flips.

"Are you seeing your ex?" he asked.

"No . . ." I paused before continuing. "I'm meeting his mom." Now, instead of flips, my stomach was in knots. I couldn't tell if he was mad or why I was so nervous to tell him. Having this conversation with Ryan felt strange. Why do I suddenly feel guilty for seeing Jeff's mom for dinner? I realized that I was subconsciously gnawing on my bottom lip so much that it started to hurt.

"That is interesting," he finally responded.

"It's not what you think," I interjected quickly.

"And what do I think?" he asked, peering into my soul.

"I don't know. Tell me."

Another five-second pause that felt like an eternity.

"Nothing."

"It doesn't feel like nothing."

"Is your ex going to be there?"

"No, just her and me. She's been reaching out for weeks, and I've been avoiding her. I feel like I owe her a conversation."

"Why? Shouldn't her son have that conversation?"

"Yeah, but it's complicated."

"I see."

"Are you okay?" I noticed he was rustling through the papers again, more distracted this time.

"Yeah, why?"

"You seem . . . concerned."

"Do I have something to be concerned about?" he asked.

"No." I paused. "But do you trust me?"

"It's the others I don't trust. But it's cool if you have to close a chapter, right?" he said sarcastically.

"Ryan." I could tell he was upset or bothered.

"Kamryn."

He looked at me and didn't say anything else, so I decided to just leave the conversation there. I probably needed to reserve my energy for Mrs. Rose tonight, anyway.

"Okay. So, I'll see you later tonight, then?" I asked.

"Sure."

"Miss you," I blurted out.

It wasn't like me to blurt out my emotions like that to anyone, especially Ryan. I caught myself holding my breath, waiting for him to acknowledge my statement. Our conversations were usually pretty light until moments like these, when my past casted a cloud over the present. I wanted him to know that there was nothing to worry about. Ryan paused from sorting through paper. He picked up the phone from where it was resting to bring it closer to his face. He gave me that dangerously devilish smile again.

"I always miss you, Kamryn. Don't be too late."

*****

I pulled up to The Pier restaurant at 6:15. The reservation was for 6:30 p.m., but Mrs. Rose was very punctual. I figured if we were both early enough, the dinner might go a little faster. I told the hostess that I was there for a reservation under the name Julia Rose. She politely turned on her heels and told me, "Right this way," as we headed to the table. Of course, Mrs. Rose is already sitting there at the best table in the restaurant. A table for two next to the window with a view of the water and the sunset. As the hostess and I approached the table, Mrs. Rose stood to greet me.

"Kamryn dear, it's so lovely to see you. How are you?"

Mrs. Rose was always so well put together and beautiful. Never a hair or line out of place. Fashionable, stylish, and always so kind. Maybe too kind to her spoiled son, but that was just her nature. I always felt she added to Jeff's behavior by enabling him. Jeff was never chastised as a child. She told me once before that she didn't believe in telling the children "No" and that kids needed to grow up and make their own decisions for themselves without being influenced by their parents. Maybe that's why Jeff was nothing like his family in personality, only resemblance.

"Hi, Mrs. Rose. It's good to see you, too."

"Since you refuse to call me 'Mom,' please at least call me Julia, dear. I wish it wasn't under such drastic circumstances that we are getting together." She rubbed my shoulders and motioned for us to sit down as she waived the waiter over.

She always insisted I call her mom or Julia, which made me uncomfortable. The waiter quickly hurried over, as if on standby for this table only.

"What can I get for you, Mrs. Rose?"

"Yes, we'll have a bottle of Antica Cabernet Sauvignon, the lobster and crab canapes, a balsamic vinaigrette salad, and Caesar salad to start. You still like Caesar salads, right, dear?"

"Yes, that's fine. Thank you." I was touched that she remembered. How is it that Jeff's mom remembers more about my likes and dislikes than he ever did, and I barely spent time with the woman?

"Will that be all, Mrs. Rose?" the waiter asked.

"Yes, dear. We're still undecided on dinner at the moment." The waiter quickly hurried off to the kitchen to deliver our order to the chef.

"So, let's have at it, dear. How are you really doing?" She gave the most heartwarming smile that she could.

"I'm doing okay. I started a new job and got a new place. Just been keeping myself busy."

"Well, I could hardly get any answers from that son of mine. Lauren called and told me when Jeff wasn't answering his phone. I must admit I was shocked that something like this could ever happen."

"Honestly, Mrs. Rose . . ." She gave me a stern look that almost resembled her son. "Sorry . . . Julia."

"Thank you, dear."

"This has been going on for a long time. This isn't the first pregnancy; let alone the first time he's cheated. I just can't be a participant in this game anymore. Jeff isn't going to change—at least, not for me, and not for us."

"I understand, dear. Relationships are hard, especially during the dark times when your spouse puts you in a difficult place and you must decide. I have been there a few times or two."

"With Mr. Rose?" I asked.

She nodded in response.

"We've been through our fair share before and after the children. It took a while for us to get pregnant, and I figured he grew tired of waiting for me. I think he always resented that I enjoyed working. I love being a mother, but it's not my only identity."

The waiter comes back to the table with our wine and appetizers, causing Julia to pause her story.

"Have you decided what you wanted for dinner, Kamryn?"

No, I hadn't. I've barely glanced at the menu. I opened it up, glimpsed over the menu quickly and saw lots of choices. Some I could barely pronounce.

"I'll have the salmon." My usual safe choice.

"That sounds lovely. I'll order salmon, as well. May I have the zucchini instead of asparagus as a side?"

"Of course, Mrs. Rose." The waiter turned to me. "Will the asparagus be okay for you, ma'am?"

"Yes, that's fine. Thank you." As soon as he hurried off to the kitchen, I continued our conversation.

"If you don't mind me asking, how did you manage to stay? Was it just for love?"

"Love? Hmph. No, dear. There are times in your life when love has nothing to do with it. I suppose I was too busy to notice at times. And when Robby was careless enough to let me find out, I would raise hell and threaten to leave. I was almost ready to leave once, and then I found out I was pregnant with Jeffrey. Then, Lauren came shortly after, and we were a family. I gave up my work for a time being while the children were little, but that didn't last long. I thought he enjoyed that, having me home twenty-four-seven to look after the home and children."

"So, you stayed for the children?" I asked, trying to get to the reason for it all.

"Yes and no. Honestly, I stayed for myself. When the times were good, they were great. Robby has his ways, but he was still an adoring husband and father. He loves his family. I think once he realized he couldn't keep me at home, he began to accept me. And I accepted him."

"You mean, you let him cheat on you knowingly?" I couldn't believe my ears.

Julia paused from her food and looked up at me.

"I let him be happy, and he let me be the same."

"Is that what you expect me to do with Jeff? Just let him cheat and disrespect me while I hold down the home front and push out babies?" Easy, Kamryn, I warned myself as my temper flared.

"No. While Robby may have had his infidelities, he wasn't idiotic enough to bring a child home. He was very careful."

"Careful? Careful because he didn't get anyone pregnant outside of his home?"

"I don't think he could if he tried, dear. You see, for a while, we thought we couldn't have children. So, we planned for Lauren, but then Jeffrey came as a surprise."

I saw the waiter approaching our table again with our dinner. I barely touched my salad after listening to Julia. The waiter removed our salad bowls and appetizer plates. As soon as he left, my mind was back to Julia.

"I'm sorry; you said you planned for Lauren. I don't understand. Jeff is older."

"Yes, Lauren was adopted. I'm sure they've told you?"

She saw the shock on my face as I shook my head.

"No, neither one ever said anything." I was stunned. Imagine being in a relationship with a man for years and not knowing that his only sibling is adopted. Not that it mattered, but it was a significant family detail that I knew nothing about. Lauren and I had been friends longer than Jeff and I had been together, and she'd failed to mention that detail, as well.

"Robby and I didn't get pregnant right away after marrying. It took quite a while, and I didn't make it any easier with my work and traveling. Robby resented me for it, and we fought and fought. I think the cheating came as a result. So, after a few years, we planned to adopt. It took a while to find a suitable family that wanted to give up their child. There weren't as many adoption programs back then, so we waited. Then, to our surprise and delight, I became pregnant with Jeffrey. We heard from an adoption agency a month before having Jeffrey. A young mother was pregnant and wanted to give her child up. She read our profile and chose us. We hesitated at first, being so close to having Jeffrey, but once we saw that beautiful little girl's face, we couldn't say no. They were born only a few days apart."

"So, you raised them as twins?" I sat in disbelief as I listened to her story. The Rose family had secrets deeper than tree roots.

"Yes." She smiled. "We saw it as a blessing to have two bundles of joy come home with us instead of one. We thought it would be easier for the children to just say they were fraternal twins rather than explain about the adoption."

"When did they find out?"

"We decided to tell them once they were teenagers. They were inseparable as kids, but Jeffrey started to act out as he got older. And Lauren started to question the differences she saw in herself from the family. So, we thought it was time to tell them the truth. But now, I wonder if we ever should have told them. Maybe we could have avoided all of this."

"I don't think knowing his sister was adopted has anything to do with Jeff's behavior. He's a grown man who makes his choices. This has nothing to do with Lauren."

"Honey, this has everything to do with Lauren. It's a family issue. I should have paid attention earlier. The signs were there that something was wrong. They were too close." Her voice trailed as she looked at her glass of wine. The bottle was nearly empty, and I hadn't finished my first glass.

"Too close? What do you mean?" Julia was obviously tipsy because she was starting not to make any sense. Something was troubling her.

"Isn't it obvious, dear? They were sleeping together. Lauren called and told me she was pregnant, and Jeffrey was the father."

I grasped the table to prevent myself from passing out. The sudden onset of dizziness was almost too much. I wanted to vomit but held it in. What did I just hear? Jeff and Lauren. Jeff and Lauren were not brother and sister by blood. They were lovers.

"What?" That's all I could get out. My mind was racing at the last thing that Julia said.

"Kamryn, dear, I thought you knew. Isn't that why you left? Why did the two of you break up?"

"I knew he was cheating, but not with Lauren." I heard my voice start to crack.

"You mentioned the pregnancy, so I thought you knew . . ."

"Knew what, Julia?! That your son is sleeping with his sister?" I said a little too loud, causing Julia to straighten her spine and look around the restaurant for any peering eyes.

"Kamryn, please," she pleaded, with a cold look I had never seen in her eyes before.

How could I miss this? I've been around this family for nearly a decade, so how could I not notice this?

"You said there were signs? What signs?"

I could tell she was hesitant to tell me anything else, considering I was on the verge of a nervous breakdown.

"After they knew about the adoption, they were distant for a while. Dr. Levine, that's our family therapist, said it was normal for teenagers to alienate themselves to process their feelings. And then, one day, it just stopped. Everything seemed to go back to normal. The kids were speaking, and there was less tension at home. Then, I saw Jeffrey coming out of Lauren's bedroom one morning. I asked him what he was doing in there, and he said he couldn't sleep. I was naïve for a while, thinking that they were just comforting each other through what Dr. Levine calls "the healing process." Then, the late-night visits to each other's rooms became more frequent. I tried to separate them by sending Lauren to a different college, but she soon followed behind Jeffrey. She told me and Robby that she was feeling homesick and thought it would be better if she went to school closer to Jeffrey. Of course, Robby bought it and arranged for her transfer. But I knew it was something more. I just didn't have the heart to confront them. Robby was never home to notice it, so he called me crazy when I mentioned it to him. I guess now, we all have to face this as a family."

"Stop. Just stop. I can't hear any more. Why are you telling me all of this?"

"I didn't realize I was telling you anything. I'm more surprised that you didn't already know half of what I'm saying right now. Obviously, I thought you knew about Lauren's pregnancy, since you two are friends."

"No. Surprisingly, she hasn't told me that she's pregnant by her brother." I grimaced.

"Well, I guess it's not an easy conversation to have."

"Julia, I need to leave. I can't deal with this right now."

"Wait. I'm sorry I upset you. That wasn't my intention. I just wanted to ask you for your discretion."

"My discretion? So, you came here to ask me to keep quiet about your family's affairs?"

"This is a family matter, and we will handle it accordingly. The last thing any of us need is public attention right now. Not until we get this all sorted out. Lauren is considering getting rid of the baby—or, at least, she will once I talk to her again, and then we can put this whole thing behind us. Maybe you can even find it in your heart to forgive Jeffrey. I'm sure he's sorry, and he loves you. I've always thought you were the best thing for him."

"Forgive him? You want me to go home and coddle your son after hearing that he's been sleeping with his *sister*, who also happens to be a friend of mine? Are you crazy?"

"No. I'm far from crazy, but I will do anything to protect my family."

"You can keep your little sick family. I want nothing to do with you or him." I grabbed my purse and headed toward the exit. Digging in my purse for my keys, I quickly realized that I'd parked with the valet. I pulled out my wallet and handed the ticket over to the valet attendant. As I waited for my car, I found my phone at the bottom of my purse. Three texts: two from Ryan and one from Mica.

Ryan: There's no one here for me to flirt with . . . ☹

Ryan: I miss you. <3

Mica: Hey. Just checking on you. Let me know if you need me to come up there . . . See you soon!

CHAPTER 27
Brotherly Love

———— ❧ ————

I didn't respond to either text. Thankfully, the valet pulled up with my car. I rushed inside so I could hide my face, almost forgetting to tip him. As soon as I sat down, the tears started to fall harder. I was crying uncontrollably with my hands on the wheel, the car still in park. Jeff was sleeping with his sister. Lauren, who is my friend, is pregnant by her brother—her adoptive brother, whom she's had an intimate relationship with for years, according to their mother. And I was the fool who knew nothing, sensed nothing, and saw nothing for all of these years. Yeah, that pretty much summed it up.

A car honked the horn behind me. It was the valet attendant, waiting for me to move so he could bring another car to the front of the line of waiting customers. I put the car in drive and pulled up a little to get out of their way as my phone buzzed again. The frequent notifications signaled that this may be a group chat. I slid across the screen to unlock the phone again.

Nicole: Is it bad that Andrew is annoying me and turning me on at the same time during this game?

Lauren: LOL! He looks like a twig crawling on the floor.

Nicole: Yeah, but I can't stop checking out his butt. Michelle, call right hand green on the next turn so I can get a better angle!

Mica: Y'all are distracting me! Next round, I'm putting you up against him, one-on-one.

Lauren: OMG . . . LOL. Kamryn, where are you, girl?

Mica: She'd better be on her way here! Enough of these secret dinners with scorned family members.

Lauren: ???

I quickly chimed in to prevent Mica from spilling the beans about my dinner with Jeff's mom.

Kamryn: OMW, ladies!

I don't want Lauren making an excuse to leave before we've had a chance to chat.

*****

I got to Mica's house eighteen minutes later, a commute that should have taken me twenty-five minutes. In between my tears, I felt a rage growing inside. I needed to calm down before I committed a crime tonight. On the drive over, I thought of several ways I would strangle Lauren and bury her and Jeff alive. How many times had they had sex while we were together? Did they have sex in our home? I recalled the times she popped in for a visit when I wasn't home, claiming that she had just missed me and she wanted to drop something off for Jeff. Usually, it was nonsense mail—family photos, old letters. Thinking back, Jeff was never a sentimental person and never cared for the personal stuff. But Lauren always had an excuse. I remember admiring the close moments that they rarely had, wishing I had siblings that I could share the same memories with.

Approaching the door, I heard the loud laughter coming from the other side. I rang the bell, and after a few seconds, Charlie came to the door with a drunken hello. He took a step back to give me a second glance, concerned for me when he saw the tears in my eyes.

"Hey . . . You don't look too good. You, okay?" Charlie asked.

I walked right past him, down the hall, and into the living room, where all of the noise was coming from. I must have looked worse than I thought because one by one, everyone started to look over towards me as silence fell over the room. Ryan stood up first and walked straight to me, placing his beer on the coffee table. He stopped in front of me and placed both hands on my arms.

"Kamryn, what's wrong? Are you okay?" Ryan asked, blocking my view of everyone.

"Kamryn. What happened?" I heard Mica approaching from behind him.

"Move," was all I could say as I moved around Ryan's tall frame and took another step into the living room. He allowed me to ease past him but kept his hands on my arm.

I scanned the room and finally made eye contact with Lauren. She was concerned like the others at first, then confused. She finally realized it: I was only looking at her. The next emotion I saw on her face was clear—fear. Lauren looked down into her drink to avoid further eye contact and the wrath that was about to meet her.

"Is it true?" I asked her, but she never looked up.

"Is what true? What's going on?" Mica asked, looking around the room for someone to answer.

I waited a few seconds to see if Lauren was going to acknowledge my question. Still nothing.

"Hello? What is going on? Kamryn, are you okay?" Nicole chimed in.

"Lauren, is it true?" I asked again.

"Is what true? Lauren, what is she asking you about?" Mica was now growing frustrated.

Lauren finally looked up at everyone in the room but not at me. I saw the tears in her eyes, but I'd grown cold towards her in the last twenty minutes on the drive over.

"Can we talk in private, Kamryn?" Her voice was just above a whisper as she attempted to hold back more tears.

"Private? I've just had to sit and listen to your mother tell me about your family affairs in public! So, no, we can't talk in private!"

"Kamryn, please," Lauren pleaded.

"Wait. Ladies, what's going on?" Mica asked, sounding more concerned than frustrated.

"Tell them, Lauren! Tell them it's not true." A part of me wanted to believe that this was all some nightmare, and I would wake up eventually—next to Ryan, of course, because Jeff would never touch me again. Ryan was still standing behind me, firmly holding my arms.

"Kamryn, I'm so sorry. I didn't mean to . . . "

"Mean to what?!" I screamed. Even her apology had me enraged.

"Kamryn, please calm down and tell us what's going on. I'm starting to freak out," Nicole interjected.

"She's pregnant!" I shouted as the room went silent again, and more confusion spread across everyone's face.

"Um, congratulations," Andrew chimed in, not knowing what else to say.

"Is that true, Lauren? How come you didn't tell us?" Mica asked.

I waited to hear Lauren's response to see if she was going to explain herself. But nothing came out except for more tears and sobbing.

"Yes, I'm pregnant," she finally confirmed after a moment.

"You don't seem so happy, girly. How come you didn't tell us? This is exciting, right?" Nicole asked.

"Because she's pregnant by her brother."

"What?!" Nicole and Mica exclaimed in unison.

Silence again, with all eyes on Lauren again. She lifted her head and wiped her face. Something was different about the look she gave me this time. It lacked remorse and empathy. She seemed pleased with herself.

"Adoptive brother, as I'm sure you just found out," she stated as she looked at me.

"Wait, what?! You're sleeping with Jeff, or is there an adoptive brother that we don't know about?" Nicole asked.

"Jeff. According to their mother, she's been sleeping with him for years," I blasted.

Lauren finally stood up and walked toward me, shoulders squared. She smirked as she approached. Ryan must have noticed the aggression in her stance, as well, because he placed his arm around my waist and held me close.

"Lauren, is this true?" Mica asked in disbelief as Lauren passed by her.

"Yes. I was adopted." She stopped a few feet away from me. Smart move. "And yes, I've been sleeping with Jeff. Are you happy now, Kamryn? Does that make you feel better to hear me say it?"

"You're a slut."

"No, I'm in love. We're in love. I'm sorry you had to find out this way, but I'm glad that you know now."

"In *love?* You little bitch!" In the next second, I was lunging at Lauren's neck. I was barely able to scratch the surface before Ryan flung me back into his arms. Mica jumped in front of Lauren to push her back towards the couch.

"You were supposed to be my friend! How could you do this?! You're fucking your brother, you back-stabbing slut!" I screamed.

"I am your friend! You have no idea about the type of person Jeff is or what he needs! I do that for him, not you. And did you ever think that you were sleeping with him behind my back?!"

"Are you insane?! We were together for seven years!" I shouted back.

"Well, I've been with him for years! Before you even were a thought, I was with him. You were just a distraction for our parents. He never loved you, Kamryn."

"This is sick. I can't believe what I'm hearing." Nicole took a seat back down on the couch.

"It's not sick. We were raised as a family, but there is no blood relation. It's perfectly normal," Lauren defended herself.

"Okay. So, it's normal to sleep with your adoptive brother and keep it a secret for years. But we're friends, Lauren. Kamryn is your friend. How could you do this to her?" Now, Mica was getting curious. Obvious of her to take my side, considering we were best friends.

"You think I wanted this? From the moment you started dating him, I asked him to call it off. I felt betrayed at first that he was dating a friend of mine. I knew there were other women, but nothing too serious, and no one this close to us before. But you were different for some reason. Our mother had started to grow suspicious, always watching us whenever we were too close. Then, one day, he mentioned to her that he was dating someone: you. It was evident from her reaction that her worst fears had been put to ease now that Jeff had a girlfriend. I tried to warn you, too, you know."

"You tried to warn me about what?" I asked curiously.

"Jeff. He's not who you think is. He's dangerous."

"So, you tried to warn me about your brother? How? By pretending you hated him all of these years?"

"Kamryn . . ." she began to speak again.

"Stop! Just shut up!" I shouted, but my voice was cracking. For years, Lauren had pretended to be disgusted by everything her brother did. The typical, "Ugh, how could you date him?" comments over the years seemed normal for a relationship between brother and sister. She never spoke highly of him and never showed admiration for anything he accomplished over the years. Instead, there was always contempt toward him.

"Kamryn . . . I'm sorry you found out this way. If it were up to me, none of this would have happened like this. But I can't take back falling in love or my baby, regardless of what anyone thinks." She looked around awkwardly, seeing all eyes were still on her.

"You know you're not the only one, right? He got another woman pregnant."

Lauren shot me a look that told me she was not pleased by her brother's little indiscretion.

"She was lying. She got pregnant by her husband and tried to say it was Jeff's baby to make her husband jealous," she answered quickly.

"Who told you that?" I asked.

"Who do you think?" Lauren replied in a snarky tone.

"Okay, ladies. This is a bit much. I think we should just call it a night," Mica interjected, advising Lauren to stop talking, but she was looking at me.

Maybe she could tell that I was about to break down and needed to be rescued. But I wasn't in the mood to be rescued. I was angry and hurt, and I wanted revenge. Before anyone could say anything, I lunged towards Lauren and tried to grab her by her neck and face but only managed to get hair in my grasp, thanks to Ryan. He suddenly had one arm wrapped around my waist and his other hand trying to control my flailing arms.

Mica and Nicole stepped in front of Lauren. I couldn't tell if they were protecting her from me or holding her back from striking me. I heard her yell that I'm a psycho as Ryan carried me towards the front door and straight to his car. He settled me next to the passenger side door, still holding me.

"Let me go!" I tried to shove his arms and make a move towards the front door again.

"No. What are you going to do? Go back in and hit a pregnant woman?"

I stopped for a minute and stared back at him. Did I actually hit her? I tried to replay the last ninety seconds in my mind. What am I doing, trying to fight a pregnant woman? What am I doing, trying to fight a friend? I can't believe I just did that in front of everyone.

"Let's go home." Ryan interrupted my thoughts and opened the car door.

There was complete silence on the ride to Ryan's house. After the stunt I'd just pulled, I couldn't tell what he was thinking about me. I was completely erratic and emotional. I looked over at Ryan, and he kept his eyes on the road. No glances, no sounds, nothing.

"Did I hit her?" I asked as I turned back to my window.

"No. I stopped you before you could."

"That's a relief."

"Yeah, it is."

"I need to call Michelle. I'm sure she's upset." I started digging through my purse again to pull out my phone.

"I'm sure she understands."

"Do you?" I asked, trying to avoid his eye contact.

"Do I what?" He finally looked at me as he turned down his street.

"Nothing. Forget it. You just seem upset."

He pulled into his driveway, turned the car off, and looked straight ahead, avoiding me.

"I'm upset that you had to go through this. Disgusted by your so-called friend for sleeping with her brother, who happens to be your ex. And I'm irritated that your ex is still causing you so much pain. You shouldn't be dealing with the consequences of his mess."

"I can't even believe this is happening," I said as I sat back in the seat.

✳✳✳✳✳

Ryan

I opened the front door and let Kamryn walk inside first. She went straight for the restroom without another word. I didn't know what my next move should be. Is she going to cry all night on my shoulder? Does she even want to be here, or would she prefer to be left alone? I headed to the kitchen and decided to open a bottle of wine. Kamryn was standing at the back door by the time I got back into the living room. She turned around as she heard me approaching.

"Figured you could use a stress reliever."

I handed her a glass and took a sip of my own. She guzzled the entire glass in a few seconds without pausing.

"You okay?" I asked.

"Yeah. Thanks."

"Should I get you another glass?"

"No, I had something else in mind." She took my glass from my hand and placed both glasses on the shelf. She turned to me and placed both arms around my neck to kiss me.

"Kamryn, what are you doing?" I pulled back so I could look at her.

"What do you think I'm doing?" She leaned back in on her tippy toes to kiss me again. This time, she was using her body weight to push me backwards towards the couch.

"Kam, you don't have to do this." I managed to grab one of her hands that was unbuttoning my shirt.

"I want to." She was being persistent.

I fell back on the couch, and Kamryn delicately slipped out of her dress and climbed into my lap to unbuckle my pants. I knew she was using me as a distraction, but I wasn't going to be able to resist her much longer. She moved her kisses from my lips to my neck, and I started to feel myself growing inside my pants.

"Baby, wait. Look at me." She paused again and looked at me, this time with tears in her eyes.

"I need you," she finally responded.

I saw the pain in her eyes. She was sitting in my lap, holding onto my manhood, but she was broken inside. Jeff had managed to disrupt her happiness and our little paradise. This was not how I envisioned our night would go, but we were here now. She didn't need to talk; she didn't need a drink; she needed to escape. She was hurting and asking me to take the pain away, even if it was only for a little while. I grabbed her by the waist, pushed myself inside of her, and held her close. She adjusted her hips, eased her body down, closed her eyes, and, for a moment, she escaped.

CHAPTER 28
Spill it, Sister

———⌘———

The next day, Ryan dropped me off at Mica's house so I could pick up my car. I didn't call her to let her know I was coming over, nor did I respond to her several calls or texts. I had every intention of just getting in my car and driving off, but as we pulled up, Mica opened her front door and stood in the doorway with her arms folded. I stared out the window, wondering how on earth she knew we were outside.

"I texted her to let her know we were on the way," Ryan stated.

"What?" My head snapped back, and looked at him in shock.

"You didn't want to talk to me about it last night, and I understand. But I think you should still talk to someone. Michelle was worried, so she texted me, and I let her know I would be bringing you here."

I stayed silent and looked back toward the window. I was unsure of how to feel that my best friend and Ryan were texting and showing concern for my well-being behind my back.

"Don't be upset, Kamryn. I know you're hurting, and I just want you to be okay."

"Thanks." I unbuckled my seatbelt and headed towards Mica.

"How on earth could you think I'd be upset or mad with you? You sound ridiculous, Kamryn. I was freaking out all night. Charlie had to stay over just to keep me calm."

"I busted up your party, embarrassed myself, and tried to kill our friend." I paused. "*Your* friend." I snorted in correction.

"You didn't bust up anything, and you have nothing to be embarrassed about. We actually think you handled that better than any of us ever could."

"We?"

"Yeah. Sorry. Charlie and I stayed up asking each other questions about how we would've responded in that situation. And trust me, your version was prettier than ours."

"Really?"

"Yeah. Charlie said he would have tried to throw his friend from the balcony if that were him." Mica chuckled.

"And you? Would you have attacked your pregnant friend?"

"Kam, honestly, I don't know. I think at that moment, who knows what any of us would do? I could see that you were spacing out, trying to process everything. Hell, I'm still trying to not think about Lauren and Jeff together. Yuck! But just because she's pregnant doesn't mean she doesn't have an ass whooping coming."

"I can't even believe this is happening. I feel so embarrassed."

"Why? You didn't hit her. Captain America made sure of that." She smirked.

"I'm embarrassed because my ex-boyfriend and my ex-friend, who happen to be brother and sister, have been sleeping together. For years! How the hell did I not see that? How didn't I notice?"

"She played us all, Kam. None of us noticed it."

She pretended to hate him for years because she was secretly in love with him."

"God, it's hard for me to hear you say that out loud," she said after a moment.

"You know what hurts the most? She's not even sorry. Did you hear her last night?" I asked while Mica nodded in acknowledgement. "She knew what she was doing all these years, watching me get played for a fool. And she stood there and defended herself. Called her actions 'love.'"

"I still can't believe it. Feels like the twilight zone."

"I don't know who is worse, Lauren or her mother."

"I never got a chance to ask you about the dinner. How did it go? I mean, besides the obvious."

"Well, it didn't go as expected."

"Sorry. You don't have to talk about it."

"No. I mean, I thought she was going to ask me about Jeff and try to convince me to get back together with him. I was all prepared to stand my ground and tell her that her son was a scumbag."

"Yeah, I think she knows."

"It never even came up. I think she thought Jeff and I broke up because I found out about Lauren and the pregnancy. She spent most of the night giving me their family history."

"So, she made excuses for this madness?" Mica looked shocked.

"Not really. She explained that there had been issues in the family for years. Before me, way before Jeff and Lauren."

"Hmph. That's putting it lightly."

"She knew, Mica."

"Knew what?" Mica sat up a little from her seat.

"She knew they were sleeping together when they were teenagers. She caught them and decided to do family therapy, which obviously didn't work."

"Wait. Stop. This is sick. Mr. Rose knew, too?"

I shrugged my shoulders in response. "I guess. I mean, how could he not?"

"Wow. This is too much for me to digest. How are you feeling now, Kam?"

"Stupid and confused. I don't know what to do next."

"I don't think there's anything for you to do, sis. Jeff is not your responsibility anymore. And clearly, Lauren isn't a friend. You don't have to do anything about their mess. Leave that for the Roses."

I nodded a little to let Mica know that I heard her, even though no words came out of my mouth.

"But if you're feeling confrontational, you don't have to do it alone."

"I'm not confronting her again. I don't trust that I won't try to kill her."

"I'm not talking about Lauren. I mean the other asshole."

"What happened after I left last night?" I had been dying to know the answer to this question . . .

"Nothing, really. We all stood around staring at each other in shock for a few minutes. Then, Lauren slowly made her exit."

"Did she say anything?" I asked.

"She said that I didn't understand. I told her that I didn't want to understand and that sleeping with her brother was her business, but being a shitty friend makes it our business."

"You didn't have to do that, Mica. You don't have to draw a line in the sand," I said, feeling grateful for her friendship.

"I know I didn't, but how could I not? None of us are perfect, but there's just some shit you don't do. There are lines that you don't cross. She and Jeff, as gross as it seems, that's not my business. They're technically not blood. But carrying around this charade for years, pretending to be a friend in your corner when she was literally sleeping with the enemy? That's a hard page to turn and just carry on like nothing happened."

"Tell me about it." Before I could stop them, the tears were falling, and I was sobbing on the sofa.

"I'm sorry, Kam Kam." Mica got up from her seat and joined me on the sofa to comfort me.

"Almost ten years of friendship, ruined." I barely understood myself through my own tears.

"Kamryn, listen to me. You didn't do this; they did. Do not allow yourself to take on their guilt. You have no fault in this."

"I know, but it hurts like hell."

We sat in silence for a few moments until the tears started to dry.

"You know what will make you feel better?"

"What?" For a second, I thought she was reading my mind and getting ready to suggest we go find Jeff and Lauren.

"Pancakes!" Mica exclaimed. I guess she wasn't a mind reader after all.

"Yeah, that does sound good."

"I bet. I can hear your stomach growling from over here."

"Is it that bad?"

"Yes. And while I cook, can you tell me how long you and Ryan have been fooling around?"

"What?" I asked, pretending to be shocked.

"I watched the way he came to your side the moment you walked through the door, how he held on to you so you didn't end up on an episode of Snapped. Then, he whisked you away like a thief in the night. Not to mention him texting me and bringing you back over to my place today."

In the heat of the moment, I didn't think anyone had noticed anything going on last night. Ryan had been so focused on me that we'd completely let our guard down in front of everyone.

"I don't know what you're . . ." I tried one last attempt to cover up my tracks with my best friend.

"Spill it, sister!"

CHAPTER 29
A Rose Revealed

—❦—

Jeff sat in his car, clenching the steering wheel, parked adjacent to the building he had followed him to last week. When he did a Google search, he couldn't find any recent locations or addresses listed, so he had to track him closely. He had done everything humanly possible to win her back. And he might have succeeded if it had not been for his cackling mother and sister. It was no one's business who he slept with, not even his parents'. It's not as if he forced this on her. Lauren wanted him; even as teenagers, she was always flaunting herself around the house. He'd watched her for years before he snuck into her room one night while his parents were out. She pretended that she had no clue what was about to happen until they were both fully naked, standing in front of each other. Seemed like so long ago, but Lauren had grown over the years. He watched her body develop right in front of his eyes, which made for great practice.

It had always been just sex for them, and Lauren knew that. It wasn't until she transferred to his college that he noticed her feelings started to change. She became jealous of other women he slept with and even threatened to tell their parents. Of course, he couldn't allow that to happen. They continued to sleep together, but it was less and less after he met Kamryn. A few years after college, she threatened to tell Kamryn if he didn't agree to be with her. Jeff didn't like to be threatened and couldn't risk losing Kamryn. Kamryn was different. She curbed his urges most of the time. He felt normal when he was with her. But he had to do something about his sister and her idle threats.

He decided to invite her over for dinner. Lauren didn't hesitate to jump at the opportunity to be alone with him. When she arrived at the house, she was glowing with love for him. Over dinner, Jeff tried to convince her again why their relationship wouldn't work. By then, they already knew about the adoption, so in Lauren's eyes, they could have a life together. But Jeff knew that in the public eye, they would always be viewed as siblings. He couldn't risk ruining his reputation or their family name.

Lauren spent most of the night trying to persuade him of why they should be together. Jeff could tell that his efforts were pointless, so he tried to reason with her to wait until the time was right. Frustrated with Jeff's tone and harshness, Lauren tearfully excused herself from the table and made an attempt to leave. Jeff quickly rushed behind her, grabbing a metal tchotchke statue from the living room table, and bashed it over her head. She blacked out immediately, so Jeff rushed to catch her before she hit the floor.

He didn't want to hurt her; he just needed to scare her. Besides, she was family.

By the time she woke up, Jeff had moved her to the room in the basement. He had her chained to the inside of his cage where he usually kept them. Jeff sat in a dark corner, watching her scream and cry for help as she panicked with complete horror.

"Don't panic," Jeff spoke calmly.

Of course, she panicked and began screaming so loudly that he had to sedate her. They hadn't had any issues since then—until now. Lauren was supposed to be on the pill, but she had obviously lied. This pregnancy complicated things. Now, he was left with no choice but to take this matter into his own hands.

Jeff sat in the car, watching Kamryn's new love interest as he recalled Lauren's screams from that night long ago. He hadn't needed to go through such drastic measures in years. Most women accepted the payout and gladly signed a non-disclosure agreement, or NDA. He usually didn't have to get involved and was able to rely on his lawyer to handle the transactions. But this one was personal. Someone was threatening his family again, and he couldn't allow that.

Jeff heard muffled noises from his trunk. She's up. Mr. Fitness would have to wait to meet him another day. He turned up the music as he watched the Lincoln pull off into traffic. He glanced in his mirror as the banging from the trunk grew louder. He turned the radio up full blast and merged onto the street.

"Don't panic, my love. It'll be over soon."

Kamryn

I had finally worked up enough courage to come to the police station and speak with the detectives handling Jenny's case with Ryan by my side. I told them that I had my suspicions about her leaving without any notice to her family or friends. It was when I mentioned the pregnancy that they grew more curious about the relationship between Jeff and her. Surprisingly, I learned that David had been a suspect once the officers discovered that Jenny had filed for a divorce preceding her disappearance. However, no arrests were made since he had been out of town and seen on every camera at the airport, which placed him out of town without a doubt.

Once they had a second name, they went to the office to question Jeff. Based on his reactions that furthered their suspicions, they were able to obtain a warrant to search the premises of the townhome we once shared. That's where they found Jenny chained to a cage inside a room in the basement. It was Jeff's martial arts room that he kept locked away. The detective found evidence that Jeff had been drugging women over the years and purposely causing miscarriages when he couldn't convince them to have an abortion. It was sickening to watch the news anchor talk about Jeff and the Rose family in a manner that had been so foreign to me.

As I sat on Ryan's couch, snuggled in his arms, I thought of all of the memories I shared with each member of the family: the laughs, the cries, the disagreements, and makeups. It hadn't been all pleasant, but it was part of who I was—my history. I was grateful to see that chapter close as Jeff was hauled away in cuffs from his office; no shame, just arrogance over his face. Ryan rubbed my arms when Jenny's face flashed across the television screen—this time, with her family and David by her side leaving the hospital. They had found her alive. I was grateful when the cops told me that they found her in time and that she would make a full recovery. I asked them if the baby was safe, and they said it was too soon to tell. I would have to follow up with her or the family. I knew that I wouldn't, but I still felt a sigh of relief that she was no longer in fear for life trapped in that basement.

The news anchor didn't mention Lauren and her pregnancy. I guess Julia Rose had done her due diligence in keeping their family business quiet. I would probably never see Lauren again to know if she kept her child or not. For her sake, it would be best to move on and start fresh. My heart ached for her. She had betrayed me and been blindly in love with a deadly Rose. Love had a tricky

341

way of making you believe the best in people even when it didn't exist.

"You okay?" Ryan asked, snapping me out of my thoughts.

"Yeah."

"Should I turn the channel?"

"Yeah. Let's watch something else. Any good movies on?"

"Well, I had something else in mind."

I looked up at him from my nestled position on the couch.

"Oh, yeah? What is that?"

He leaned in to kiss me on the lips with my face in his hands. Yeah, love could make you see the best in people, even when it didn't exist. But it could also save you from sliding into a dark abyss. This time, I was grateful for this love.

"Let's make a movie of our own," he said softly as we drifted off into our perfect peace.

www.ingramcontent.com/pod-product-compliance
Lightning Source LLC
Chambersburg PA
CBHW081016120626
46546CB00010B/3178